OPPORTUNITIES

in

P9-CSC-795

4/18/06
13.95

Medical Imaging
Careers

REVISED EDITION

CLIFFORD J. SHERRY

McGraw·Hill

New York   Chicago   San Francisco   Lisbon   London   Madrid   Mexico City
Milan   New Delhi   San Juan   Seoul   Singapore   Sydney   Toronto

Library of Congress Cataloging-in-Publication Data

Sherry, Clifford J.
    Opportunities in medical imaging careers / by Clifford J. Sherry. — Rev. ed.
       p.   cm.
    ISBN 0-07-145871-9 (alk. paper)
    1. Diagnostic imaging—Vocational guidance.   2. Medical technologists—
Vocational guidance.   I. Title.

  RC78.7.D53S45   2006
  616.07'54'071—dc22   2005023851

1 2 3 4 5 6 7 8 9 0   DOC/DOC   0 9 8 7 6

ISBN 0-07-145871-9

Interior design by Rattray Design

McGraw-Hill books are available at special quantity discounts to use as premiums and sales promotions, or for use in corporate training programs. For more information, please write to the Director of Special Sales, Professional Publishing, McGraw-Hill, Two Penn Plaza, New York, NY 10121-2298. Or contact your local bookstore.

This book is printed on acid-free paper.

CONTENTS

FOREWORD

I BELIEVE THAT one of the most rewarding occupations is that of the radiologic technologist, the person who operates modern medical imaging equipment such as CT, MRI, nuclear medicine, ultrasound, and other scanners. I can remember, after having invented and built the first whole-body CT scanner, convincing my first radiologic technologist to learn about CT and to run my machine. At first he was hesitant about using such a new and previously unheard-of device, but after a short time he became fascinated with my new instrument, and he made a career of not only using the machine, but of teaching other technologists about the use of CT scanners. His name was Charlie Seijo, and he's still in the field. That was almost twenty years ago, and during those two decades, this imaging revolution in medicine that I started has spread throughout the world.

Today each of many hundreds of thousands of scanners in use depends on the services of several knowledgeable and skilled radiologic technicians. Being able to run one of those machines is rewarding; viewing the images that you made with the machine is rewarding; knowing that your images can often pinpoint the medical diagnosis of the patient's ills, and frequently save the patient's life, is rewarding. In fact, just working at the high end of advanced technological development is in itself rewarding.

Being a radiologic technologist requires constant learning throughout your career. There are always new improvements to the scanners in this ever-evolving field, new medical diagnoses, and new methods for scanning patients. If you like doing things by rote, this is not the field for you; but if you enjoy learning about the new and latest in technology, if being at the forefront of medical developments excites you, then this is definitely for you. Good luck, and may you never have a dull moment!

Robert S. Ledley
Chairman, Computerized Medical Imaging Society
Professor, Georgetown University
Inductee, National Inventor's Hall of Fame

Acknowledgments

I WOULD LIKE to thank my wife, Nancy, who helped edit and proof this book. Without her help and encouragement, this book could not have been written.

INTRODUCTION

A REVOLUTION IS happening in medicine, and you can be part of it. Medical imaging began with the discovery of X-rays by Wilhelm Konrad Roentgen on November 5, 1895, and the growth and development of the field continue to this day. In fact, improvements to and refinements of existing imaging technologies and discovery of new technologies will undoubtedly continue well into the twenty-first century. These techniques will provide an ever clearer and more detailed window into the body and its functions. Perhaps the most exciting area is imaging the brain, to gain a further understanding of the connection between activity in the brain and behavior.

These technologies include sonography, computed tomography, and magnetic resonance imaging, which have been in use for quite some time. They also include newer techniques, such as positron emission tomography and single-photon emission computerized tomography.

With the appropriate training and experience, you can help shape the future of medical imaging. In this book is the basic information you will need to assess your interest in and aptitude for this exciting and ever-evolving field. The book also lists programs that will provide you with the training required for your chosen area. The promise of the future is yours. Enjoy it!

1

Windows into the Body and Mind

Max Beerbohm, 1872–1956, an English essayist and caricaturist, said, ". . . the eyes are the windows of the soul." That may be true. But what is also true is that today, we can rightly claim to have "windows" into the brain.

The human brain is not particularly impressive looking. It is about the size of two fists held together, its surface wrinkled and grayish, and it has the consistency of slightly overcooked Jell-O. But despite its appearance, virtually everyone agrees that the human brain is the most complex system in the known universe. Beyond that, many people believe that the mind is more than the sum total of the chemical and electrical activity of the brain. Whether or not that is true, the brain, especially the cerebral cortex, is certainly the destination of our senses and the originator of our movements. It is also the seat of intelligence, creativity, memory, language, and other functions uniquely human. Many of these functions are found in both cerebral hemispheres. But, one of the unique features of the human brain is anatomical specialization. By this we mean that the part of the cerebral cortex dealing with language is found in one or the other cerebral hemisphere, but typically not in both.

Historical Limitations and Modern Developments

In the eighteenth, nineteenth, and twentieth centuries, basic and clinical scientists who were studying the brain and its functions mostly examined the effects of lesions and chemical or electrical stimulation in lower animals—from invertebrates to nonhuman primates. For obvious ethical reasons, the study of human brain function in normal individuals was limited to using noninvasive techniques, such as recording the electrical activity of the nervous system through use of the electroencephalogram. The exception was with humans who were born with or who had acquired (as in an accident) some damage to their brain that was manifested in their behavior. In this case, when the person died, an autopsy was performed, and it was noted what part of the brain was damaged, thus developing a relatively crude relationship between a particular part of the brain and behavior.

This all changed in the early 1990s with the development of Blood Oxygen Level Dependent functional Magnetic Resonant Imaging, commonly called BOLD fMRI. This technique was essentially noninvasive, and it allowed images of the brain with a temporal resolution of about one hundred milliseconds and a special resolution of one to two millimeters. This meant that the parts of the brain that were involved with cognitive events could potentially be identified and studied.

It is important to note that from the time the MRI was introduced (see Chapter 2) until the development of BOLD fMRI, the MRI was used as a diagnostic tool to provide physicians and other clinicians with an extraordinarily detailed peek into the anatomy of the body—better than ordinary X-rays and even CAT scans. The imaging allowed these clinicians to identify and differentiate normal and pathological tissue. Normally an MRI scan was used as a diagnostic tool when someone had a problem, and generally people had only one or a few scans in their lifetimes.

Some Applications of Research

When BOLD fMRI is used as a research tool, it is likely that "normal" individuals might be exposed to the MRI from several to many times during a research project. It is also likely that the subjects of many of these studies will be college or medical school students. The BOLD fMRI system works because deoxygenated hemoglobin is magnetic, while oxygenated hemoglobin is not. Therefore, an area of the brain with more oxygenated blood will cause the image to be more intense. A basic assumption of this technique is that if an area of the brain is more active, it will contain more oxygenated blood when compared to a time when the area is less active. A basic caveat states that there is a three-to-six-second time lag between when a brain area is activated and when increased blood flow to it can be detected. The typical BOLD fMRI protocol has several periods of activation alternating with periods of rest.

Jay N. Giedd of the National Institute of Mental Health provides one of the first, if not *the* first, glimpses into changes in the brain that occur during development. Over time he has scanned the brains of ninety-five healthy male and sixty-six healthy female brains. He found that by six years of age, a child's brain is approximately 90 percent of its adult size. The changes in the size of the head from four to eighteen years of age are due to increases in the thickness of the skull, not to brain size. The white matter, which is made up of neuronal processes, increases in roughly a linear manner. The gray matter, which consists of nerve cell bodies in the cerebral cortex, shows regional variation in growth. The frontal gray matter peaks at about 11 years of age in girls and 12.1 years in boys, while the temporal gray matter peaks at 16.7 years in girls and 16.2 years in boys.

Consider taking a look into our collective unconsciousness, as did Elizabeth Phelps of New York State University and Mahzarin Banaji of Yale. These researchers were interested in the neural basis of racial evaluation. Their subjects, a total of fourteen white males and females, were placed in an MRI scanner and shown pictures of unfamiliar white and black male faces with neutral expressions. The subjects were asked to press one button when the picture was the same as the preceding picture and another button if the picture was different. While the subjects made these evaluations, the blood flow to their amygdalae was evaluated. The amygdala is a small (about the size of the tip of your little finger) subcortical structure that is thought to be involved with emotional learning and evaluation. After the imaging session, the subjects were asked to participate in three behavioral tasks. The first was the Implicit Association Test, which reportedly measures the automatic association of positive and negative qualities of black and white social groups. The measure is based on the time it takes to respond to the following types of pairings:

(black + good / white + bad) versus (black + bad / white + good)

The second task involved a measure of the startle response while viewing unfamiliar black and white faces. The startle response is reportedly greater in the presence of stimuli that are considered more negative.

The third task was an evaluation of the expressed attitudes toward race using the Modern Racism Scale.

There was no correlation between amygdala activation and the conscious racial attitudes assessed by the Modern Racism Scale. There was a correlation between activation of the amygdala and the test of association between race (black-white) and evaluation (good-bad) and the degree that the subjects were startled in the presence of black versus white faces. These two tasks were not under the conscious control of the subject.

In a second experiment, new subjects were exposed to the images of famous and well-liked white and black individuals. In this case there was no correlation between the degree of activation of the amygdala and either behavioral task or the modern racism scale.

This suggests that while conscious evaluations of blacks by whites is increasingly positive, implicit or unconscious evaluations continue to be negative. Such evaluations can affect behavior in subtle and unconscious ways.

Consider another example. The United States is apparently in the grip of an epidemic, one that does not seem to involve the rest of the world. This epidemic concerns school-age children, even preschool children as young as four years old. It is called attention deficit hyperactivity disorder (ADHD) or attention deficit disorder (ADD). Unfortunately, there are no objective diagnostic criteria to determine if a child or adult actually has ADHD or ADD, and it is difficult to determine if a treatment is successful or not. The treatment typically consists of powerful psychostimulants, such as

Ritalin (methylphenidate), or Adderall (a mixture of dextroamphetamine and amphetamine).

BOLD fMRI may help scientists both understand the underlying condition and help evaluate the effects of stimulant treatments. D. D. Langleben and colleagues at the Department of Psychiatry, University of Pennsylvania School of Medicine, used twenty-two prepubescent boys with ADHD and seven healthy volunteers as their subjects. They noted that a brief discontinuation of treatment with methylphenidate in the boys with ADHD showed an increase in activity in the motor cortex and in the anterior cingulated cortex. This suggests that these brain areas may be involved in this disorder and that stimulant treatment may affect the function of these areas to decrease hyperactivity and increase attention span.

In another interesting study, Langleben and colleagues demonstrated increased activity in several brain areas when those subjects were being deceptive. These areas included the anterior cingulated cortex, the superior frontal gyrus, the left pre-motor and motor cortices, and the left anterior parietal cortex. This may provide an objective method that would be more accurate than the polygraph for detecting deception, because it depends on detecting the stress associated with being deceptive.

"How do I love thee, let me count the ways." Infatuation, which often precedes romantic love, brings on uncharacteristic behaviors and wild mood swings. Infatuation and the behaviors it causes have been until recently the province of poets and song lyricists. But this is no longer the case. Dr. Helen Fisher of Rutgers University and colleagues claim that they can identify the parts of the brain that are activated when one is infatuated. Surprisingly, or perhaps not so surprisingly, they are the same parts of the brain that are activated by drives like hunger, thirst, or drug cravings.

These scientists imaged the brains of young college students that were in the throes of a new love. They were shown the images of their new love while their brains were being scanned. These brain images were compared to those obtained when the students were shown the image of an acquaintance. The hot spots shown on the brain scan obtained when looking at a new love were deep in the brain, in areas of the brain that are probably below conscious awareness. Two prominent areas were the caudate nucleus (a relatively large nucleus located in the front part of the brain in the frontal lobes) and the ventral tegmental area (a small, but important area of nerve cells located near the base of the brain). These two structures communicate with each other as part of a larger circuit.

It is likely that these types of studies that attempt to correlate brain function with behavior will continue and increase. This will be coupled with an increased demand for more powerful MRI equipment to increase spatial resolution of the image and decrease the time required to obtain an image.

Thus BOLD fMRI may actually supply a window to the mind, and, ultimately, help us to understand the most complex system in the known universe. Ourselves!

2

History of Medical Imaging

Wilhelm Conrad Roentgen was born on March 27, 1845, in Lennep, in the lower Rhine Province in Germany. When he was three years old, his family moved to Apeldoorn in the Netherlands, where he attended the Institute of Martinus Herman van Doorn. He did not yet show any special aptitude, except perhaps for making mechanical contrivances.

Roentgen entered a technical school at Utrecht, but he was expelled (apparently unfairly) for drawing a caricature of one of his teachers. He entered the University of Utrecht in 1865 to study physics, but he did not have the credentials required for a regular student. When he heard that the Polytechnic at Zurich allowed students to enter by passing an examination, he took and passed the test and began studies in mechanical engineering. He attended lectures given by Rudolf Julius Emmanuel Clausius and August Adolph Eduard Eberhard Kundt, both of whom exerted great influence on his professional development.

Roentgen graduated with a Ph.D. from the University of Zurich in 1869 and was appointed as an assistant to Kundt, with whom he moved first to Wurzburg and then to Strasbourg. Roentgen's first published work dealing with the specific heat of gases was published in 1870, followed in a few years by a paper dealing with the thermal conductivity of crystals. He qualified as a lecturer at Strasbourg University in 1874, was appointed to a professorship at the Academy of Agriculture at Hohenheim in Wurtemberg in 1875, and returned to Strasbourg as professor of physics in 1876. By 1879 he had moved to the chair of physics at the University of Giessen and returned to the University of Wurzburg in 1888, where he joined such notable figures as Hermann Ludwig Ferdinand von Helmholtz and Hendrik Antoon Lorentz. He moved to the University of Munich in 1900 and remained there for the rest of his life.

Discovery of X-Rays

It was at Wurzburg in 1895 where he made his famous discovery. Roentgen was working on experiments dealing with cathode rays, which occur when an electric current is passed through a gas at extremely low pressure. He was particularly interested in the luminescence that these rays set up in certain chemicals. On November 5, 1895, he was working in a darkened room and had enclosed the cathode ray tube in a thin cardboard tube. While working, he noted a flash of light that did not come from the tube. He looked up and saw that a paper coated with barium platinocyanide, one of the luminescent substances, and some distance away, was glowing. The cathode rays, which were blocked by the cardboard tube, could not have reached the paper.

It is interesting to speculate. What would you have done if you had been in Roentgen's shoes? Would you have ignored the glowing paper and turned back to your original experiment? If so, then you would have missed the opportunity to make a major discovery. If Roentgen had turned back to his original experiment, would someone else have discovered and characterized these mysterious waves? Probably, perhaps even certainly, but, then, perhaps not. And even if someone else discovered them, when would the discovery have taken place? For example, when Sir William Crookes, the inventor of the cathode ray tube, heard of Roentgen's discovery, he realized that he had observed X-rays before Roentgen, but he just did not know it.

Fortunately, Roentgen was a curious fellow, and he turned the tube off and noted that the paper darkened. He turned it back on and it glowed. He walked into the next room and turned the tube on and noted again that the paper glowed. At this point, he decided that some sort of radiation was coming from the cathode ray tube. This radiation was highly penetrating and invisible to the eye. It would pass through a considerable thickness of paper and even through thin pieces of metal. He had no idea about the nature of this form of radiation. So, he called it an *X-ray*, the name we still use today.

Roentgen knew he was on to something and wanted to publish his results before someone else beat him to it. But, he knew he needed more data. So, for the next seven weeks he experimented furiously. In one experiment, he had his wife hold her hand over a photographic plate and exposed it to X-rays. When he developed the plate he discovered an image of his wife's hand, which showed the shadows of the bones in her hand and the ring on her finger. The bones were surrounded by the penumbra of flesh, which was more permeable to the X-rays and threw a fainter shadow. This was the first ever Roentgenogram—or X-ray.

Roentgen submitted his first paper on December 28, 1895, to the Wurzburg Physico-Medical Society, where he announced his discovery and reported on all of the fundamental properties of these waves. He was basically a shy man who preferred to work alone. He built most of the apparatuses he used in his experiments. According to popular folklore, when Roentgen was asked what he thought when he discovered X-rays, he is said to have replied, "I did not think, I experimented."

If you are interested, you can read this paper at www.emory.edu/x-rays/century_05.htm. He called the paper, "On a New Kind of Ray, A Preliminary Communication." Roentgen sent copies of his paper and some X-ray photos to a number of renowned physicists on January 1, 1896. The popular media spread the news. The first story appeared in *Die Presse* on January 5, 1896, and in the *London Standard* on January 6, 1896. The X-ray phenomenon swept through Europe and America, and in the year following Roentgen's publication of his paper, almost one thousand scientific papers and as many as forty-nine books were published describing X-rays.

The first public lecture on X-rays was given by Roentgen on January 23, 1896. During this lecture, he called for a volunteer, and Rudolf Albert von Kolliker, a Swiss anatomist and physiologist who was eighty years old at the time, had his hand X-rayed.

When X-rays pass through tissue on the way to a photographic plate, they cast a shadow. Bones appear white on black. Metal objects also appear white. Within four days after the news of X-rays reached the United States, X-rays were used to locate a bullet in the leg of a patient. It took a number of years to discover that X-rays were potentially dangerous and could cause cancer and mutations.

Roentgen shared the Rumford Medal of the Royal Society with Philipp Eduard Anton von Lenard, his mentor, in 1896. Roentgen received the first Nobel Prize in physics in 1901 for his discovery of X-rays. The unit of radiation exposure or intensity was named in his honor in 1928. It is called the Roentgen (R). Lenard received the Nobel Prize in 1905 for his discovery of cathode rays. Unfortunately, Lenard's reputation was tarnished later in life because he was one of the few important German scientists to support Hitler and the Nazis.

Roentgen never attempted to patent any aspect of X-ray production or to make any financial gain from his discovery. The inflationary period following World War I impoverished many Germans, including Roentgen. He died in relatively straitened circumstances in Munich on February 10, 1923, of a carcinoma of the intestine.

Moving X-Rays

Thomas Edison began experimenting with X-rays shortly after hearing about Roentgen's discovery. Edison had trouble obtaining X-ray tubes, so he made his own. Some of these early tubes were essentially modified electric lightbulbs. Edison's work with X-rays was wide-ranging, but he focused most of his efforts on improving the methods used for viewing X-rays, where a screen coated with a fluorescent material replaced the photographic film. He reportedly tested more than eighteen hundred materials before finally settling on calcium tungstate. In March 1896, Edison incorporated a screen coated with this material into the Vitascope. Renamed the *fluoroscope*, this device became the standard tool that physicians used to view X-rays, particularly since it allowed movements of bones and organs.

In the late 1940s and early 1950s, virtually every shoe store that sold shoes to children had a shoe-fitting X-ray unit. The dominant company in this area was the Adrian X-ray Company of Milwaukee, Wisconsin. The machine was designed by Brooks Stevens. It consisted of an X-ray tube mounted near the floor and a fluorescent screen. The X-rays penetrated the shoes and feet and presented an image of them on the screen. Most of these machines had three ports, one for the customer, one for the customer's parent, and one for the salesperson. The dangers associated with these machines were recognized as early as 1950; by 1970 they were effectively banned in thirty-three states and strictly regulated in the remaining states.

Improvements

Dr. William Herbert Rollins, a Boston dentist, working between 1896 and 1904 developed a number of devices to minimize the risk of X-ray burns. These devices included a collimator, which was designed to restrict the X-ray beam by a diaphragm and leaded tube housings. He also was instrumental in developing high voltage tubes to limit patient dose and improving the diagnostic quality of X-rays by inserting a leather or aluminum filter.

X-ray machines would have remained a laboratory curiosity were it not for H. C. Snook and his invention of the interrupterless transformer (1907) and W. D. Coolidge of the General Electric Company and his invention of the hot-cathode X-ray tube (1913). Other developments, such as the use of cellulose nitrate film base (1916–18), soluble iodine compounds as contrast media (1919–21), and the Potter-Bucky grid, which increases image sharpness (1921), all helped move X-rays out of the laboratory and into the hands of physicians.

By the 1930s virtually every hospital in the United States had some sort of X-ray equipment. Improvements such as xeroradiography and automatic film processing appeared in the 1950s.

Conventional X-rays are essentially like photographs taken with a conventional camera, except that the operative agent is X-rays rather than light waves. They can provide an accurate picture of bones, but soft tissues in a structure such as the chest are all shown with approximately equal clarity.

Computed Tomographic Scanner: A New Approach

Computed tomography (CT) or computer axial tomography (CAT) scanners work in the same manner, but the photographic plate that is used in conventional X-rays is replaced by a detector whose output is connected to a computer. The process by which a CT scanner produces a cross-sectional image is quite complicated and requires a good deal of knowledge and understanding of physics, engineering, mathematics, and computer science. The computer uses a series of mathematical equations (algorithms) to use the output of the detector and the location of the patient to reconstruct the visual image that is transmitted to a television monitor, where it can be photographed for later examination.

Mr. Godfrey Hounsfield at the EMI Corporation (the people who recorded the Beatles!) began work on a CT scanner in 1968. The initial device was built at a laboratory in Hayes, England, and used an americium isotope as the source of gamma rays. Using simple phantoms (spheres, and so forth), it took this device nine days to scan the object and two and a half hours to process a single image. The gamma-ray source was replaced with an X-ray tube, and this reduced the scan time to nine hours. For his work on the CT scanner, Hounsfield shared the 1979 Nobel Prize in medicine with Dr. Allan M. Cormack. Dr. Cormack worked in South Africa in the physics department of the University of Cape Town and in the radiology department at the Groote Schuur Hospital; he independently developed the algorithms associated with scanners.

The first prototype unit was prepared and installed for clinical studies of the brain in the Atkinson Morley Hospital near Wimbledon in 1972. The first three production units of a CT scanner, called the Mark I, were installed at the Mayo Clinic in Rochester, Massachusetts General Hospital in Boston, and Presbyterian–St. Luke's Hospital in Chicago. Mallinckrodt Institute of Radiology made history as the first institution to have two CT scanners. The Mark I was limited to scanning of the head because of the long scan time—four and a half minutes—and because it was necessary to eliminate any air gap between the scanner and the anatomical object. An air gap would attenuate the X-ray signal.

The Mark I utilized an X-ray beam that was collimated to a pencil beam and two detectors that were rigidly coupled by means of a yoke. The source-detector makes one sweep or translation across the patient, and the internal structures of the body attenuate the X-ray beam according to their density. The result is called a *view*. A total of 180 translations are performed, each separated by one degree.

The second-generation scanner, called the EMI 5000, was made available in the summer of 1975. The 5000 series scanner could complete a scan in eighteen seconds. It produced the first images of the chest and abdomen. The 5000 series utilized a ten-degree fan beam and thirty detectors. The source-detector scanned across the patient and produced thirty views with approximately one-third of a degree of angular difference between views obtained by neighboring detectors. The source-detector would then rotate ten degrees and repeat the process. This required only eighteen rotational movements.

General Electric, Siemens, Toshiba, Elscint, and Shimadzu began marketing third-generation scanners in 1975. In these scanners, the source-detector array pivots around the patient in a single rotational movement. Depending on the manufacturer, the X-ray tube is either pulsed or on continuously. Typical scan times are two to four seconds.

Fourth-generation scanners became available in the late 1970s. In these scanners the X-ray tube rotates, but the detector remains stationary. Although this requires more detectors, because the X-ray tubes have very little inertial mass, extremely fast scan times are possible.

Magnetic Resonance Imaging

The nuclei of hydrogen, phosphorus, sodium, potassium, and fluorine atoms spin on their axes, much like tiny subatomic tops. Carbon 13, which makes up about 1.1 percent of the carbon in the body, also spins in the same way. The movement of the positively charged protons (and neutrons that contain charged quarks) in the nuclei of these atoms produces magnetic fields. So, the spinning nuclei act as tiny magnets. In an applied magnetic field, these tiny atomic magnets tend to align in specific directions, usually in the same or opposite direction as the field. However, the alignment is never exact, and the nuclear magnets precess (wobble) in the direction of the field, much like a spinning top wobbles in the earth's gravitational field. These nuclei resonate with the applied field.

If an applied magnetic field that is oscillating at the same frequency that the nuclei are precessing about the steady magnetic field, then the nuclei all flip to one state or another (i.e., the same or opposite direction of the applied field). When the oscillating field is removed, the nuclei flip back to the original state. When this flip occurs, the nuclei release a small amount of energy. The nuclei become tiny radio transmitters. If a suitable coil (antenna) is present, it can detect this energy.

Scientists found that magnetic resonance could be used for imaging because magnetic resonance information could be used to code information about small units of tissue, and this information could be used to create an image. By 1974 scientists had produced a nuclear magnetic resonance (NMR) proton image of a dead mouse. The first human *in vivo* (living tissue in a living body) NMR image was produced in 1977.

By applying a broad sweep of frequencies, George Radda and his colleagues in the Department of Biochemistry at Oxford and engineers at the Oxford Instruments Group and the Oxford Research Systems developed the surface coil in 1980. The surface coil consists of a few turns of wire about a centimeter in diameter. This coil influences the nuclei in a small volume of tissue, approximately the same area as the coil and as deep as the coil's radius. This allowed Radda and his colleagues to study the phosphorus spectra in different parts of an anaesthetized rat. They chose phosphorus because it is part of the ATP (adenosine triphosphate) molecule that stores energy that is released during metabolism of food until it is needed.

By 1982–83 Radda and his colleagues, using large superconducting magnets with a clear bore of twenty centimeters, could study the phosphorus spectra *in vivo* in the arm muscles of normal human volunteers. The muscles could be at rest, exercising, or recovering from exercise. Radda's group could distinguish the various forms of phosphate that were present. During the same time period, scientists were also studying phosphorus metabolism in human babies.

Dr. Robert Schulman and his colleagues at Yale University studied carbon 13 metabolism *in vivo* in humans. They utilized glucose labeled with carbon 13 to follow glucose metabolism in the liver.

Dr. Radda set up the first clinical MRI facility at the John Radcliffe Hospital in Oxford in 1983. There scientists used a system built by Oxford Research Systems and studied the liver, brain, and heart, as well as muscles. At about the same time, Dr. P. A. Bottomley's team developed the DRESS (depth-resolved spectroscopy) techniques. The problem with these techniques was that they provided spatial information in only one dimension—depth below the surface.

In contrast to CT scanning, the MRI does not use ionizing radiation, but it does use very strong magnetic fields that may cause potential problems for individuals with (older) cardiac pacemakers or implanted ferromagnetic clips.

MRI presents anatomically correct images that can be used for localization, targeting, and navigation. MRI can also be used to study physiologic parameters such as diffusion, tissue perfusion, and flow, and these phenomena can be used to further define anatomical details. MRI can also be used for guiding biopsies and tumor resection, where its greatest advantage over CT and fluoroscopy is that it does not expose the patient to ionizing radiation. In 1995 Dr. D. Gronemeyer of the Institute of Diagnostic and Interventional Radiology (at the University of Witten/Herdecke, Mulheim/Ruhr, Germany) and his colleagues performed the first interventional procedure in using an open MRI system. The GE 0.5 T Signa SP is an MRI system with a midfield intra-operative area. The system has a vertical gap between two vertically oriented magnets. The physician sits or stands in the gap and can perform percutaneous, interventional, endoscopic, and open surgical procedures. One of the most challenging aspects of interventional MRI is the development of nonmagnetic equipment and tools.

One of the key uses of interventional MRI is in guiding and imaging thermal surgery. Using focused ultrasound, surgeons can use MRI imaging to help restrict energy deposition to the target tissue and to signal the irreversible phase transition in the target tissue.

Ultrasound

Normal adult humans can hear sounds (pressure changes in the air) that range in frequency from 20 to 20,000 hertz (Hz). One hertz is equal to one cycle per second. Any frequency higher than 20,000 Hz is commonly called *ultrasound*. Bats and certain insects can produce and hear sounds that are as high as 120 kHz (k = kilo = 1,000, so 120 kHz = 120,000 Hz).

The first man-made ultrasound did not appear until 1880, when Jacques and Pierre Curie demonstrated the piezoelectric effect at the Sorbonne in Paris. Pierre, who was twenty-one at the time of this discovery, was already an accomplished experimental and theoretical physicist. Eighteen years later, he would collaborate with his wife, Marie, in the discovery of radium. Roentgen also did some experiments with high frequency sound but stopped these experiments when he discovered X-rays.

The piezoelectric effect occurs when certain crystals, such as quartz, tourmaline, and Rochelle salt (sodium potassium tartrate), change the distribution of electric charge when they are subjected to mechanical stress. The first practical use of ultrasonics occurred during World War II, when SONAR (*SO*und *N*avigation *A*nd *R*anging) was developed to detect submarines. The basic operating principle of SONAR is relatively straightforward. A beam of ultrasound is transmitted from the surface ship into the depths of the ocean. If this sound intersects a submarine (or other submerged object), a small amount of the ultrasound is reflected back to the surface and detected. The time required for the ultrasound to travel to the submarine and back to the surface is directly proportional to the distance between the submarine and the surface ship. Diagnostic ultrasound is based on this same principle.

Medical Ultrasonic Imaging

The frequency of medical ultrasonic devices varies from 1 to 10 MHz (M = mega = 1,000,000, so 1 MHz = 1,000,000 Hz). The frequency and the wavelength of sound, including ultrasound, are inversely proportional. That is, as frequency goes up, wavelength goes down. The ability to resolve small objects is directly related to wavelength. So, high frequency ultrasonics (10 MHz) allows better resolution than low frequency ultrasonics (1–2 MHz). Unfortunately, as frequency increases, so does absorption of ultrasonic sound, so high frequency ultrasound results in shallow penetration. Therefore, higher frequency ultrasonic transducers are used for small structures, such as the eye, while lower frequency ultrasonic transducers are used for abdominal examinations. Typically as frequency increases, its dispersion from the source decreases; that is, the beam becomes more collimated.

A *transducer* is a device that converts energy from one form to another. The transducer used in ultrasonic equipment converts electrical energy into sound energy and sound energy back into electrical energy. If a piezoelectric crystal is subjected to an electric signal that oscillates at a high frequency, the crystal will expand and contract at the same frequency. The crystal face acts much like the speaker cone in a high-fidelity speaker. The crystal face vibrates rapidly, which produces sound at the same frequency. These vibrations are coupled to the skin of the patient. Coupling gel or oil is used to eliminate air. When the ultrasound waves encounter any changes in the characteristic impedance within the body, such as might occur at the interface of two different tissues, echoes are reflected back to the piezoelectric transducer. These reflections—sounds—cause the crystal face to rapidly vibrate. The mechanical energy is converted into electric energy by the crystal. The crystals are very delicate. A 2.5 MHz crystal is only 0.31 millimeter thick.

The most common scan is called the *B-scan* (brightness mode), where the emitted pulses are scanned across a plane and the echoes are displayed in two dimensions.

It has been estimated that as many as 40 percent of all pregnant women in the United States have at least one B-scan ultrasound assessment. Since the fetus's head, trunk, and limbs can be visualized, an obstetrician can determine if the fetus is suffering from abnormalities or growth retardation. Ultrasound examinations can also help determine if there is more than one fetus. It can also be used to determine the sex of the fetus. Further, ultrasound images help an obstetrician to guide a needle into the amniotic sac to withdraw fluid/cells that will help him or her determine if the fetus has certain birth defects.

Doppler Ultrasonic Scanners

Doppler ultrasonic scanners can be used to detect movement, such as blood flow. This technique depends on the fact that when a moving target reflects the ultrasonic rays, there is a Doppler-shift in the frequency of the reflected waves. For example, if a 3MHz wave is back-scattered by blood flowing in the direction of the ultrasonic beam and the blood is traveling at one meter per second, the Doppler-shift will be about 4 kHz.

Safety First! Or Perhaps Second?

Thomas Edison, William J. Morton, and Nicola Tesla were among the first to suggest that X-rays and fluorescent substances might be dangerous. Edison, a prolific inventor, might have gone on to invent other X-ray–related devices—but for one incident. One of his assistants and longtime friends, Clarence Dally, received a serious X-ray burn. The burn was severe enough to cause the amputation of both arms and ultimately his death in 1904. Dally is generally counted as the first X-ray fatality in the United States. The American physicist, Elihu Thomson, exposed the little finger of his left hand to an X-ray tube for several days for a half an hour a day. This caused pain, swelling, stiffness, erythema, and blistering. This convinced Thomson and others that X-rays were potentially very dangerous. Dr. William Herbert Rollins demonstrated that X-rays could kill adult guinea pigs and kill the fetus of a pregnant guinea pig.

Rome Vernon Wagner, an X-ray–tube manufacturer, proposed that a person who might be exposed to X-rays should carry a photographic plate in his or her pocket. The plate was developed each day to determine if exposure to X-rays had occurred. This is the forerunner of the film badge that is commonly used today.

The British Roentgen Society was formed in 1915, and the American Roentgen Ray Society was formed in 1922 and began to provide radiation protection recommendations.

3

EDUCATION AND CERTIFICATION

IF YOU ARE considering a career in medical imaging, it is a good idea to visit an imaging center in a hospital or clinic and talk to several of the professionals who are employed there. They can provide you with many insights and information about the field.

The place to begin to plan for a career in medical imaging is in high school. A typical high school curriculum that would help prepare a student for this career should include one year each of biology, chemistry, and physics; two to three years of mathematics; two years of social studies, including psychology, if possible; and four years of English. The United States is becoming more culturally diverse with each passing year, and three to four years of foreign language will help you understand members of other cultures. Electives (four to eight courses) should include computer science, if available, as well as additional courses in science and mathematics, as available.

Check with a guidance counselor or advisor to determine the general entrance requirements for professional training programs that you are interested in. It is best to pursue a program that is accredited by the Committee of Allied Health Education and Accreditation (CAHEA) of the American Medical Association (AMA). A list of currently accredited programs for nuclear medicine technologists, radiologic technologists, and sonographers are given in Appendixes A, B, and C, respectively. It is important to note that new programs are added and old programs deleted from this list. So, it is best to check the current edition of the *Allied Health Education Directory*, published annually by the CAHEA. Additional information can be obtained from the professional or registration/certification organizations listed in Appendix D.

CT/MRI

There are currently no license, certification, or registration requirements necessary to work as a CT or MRI technologist. However, many technologists hold certifications or registrations in other paramedical fields, such as medical technology or nursing and especially radiologic technology (radiographer). The credentialing agency is the American Registry of Radiologic Technologists (ARRT). The ARRT provides advanced-level examinations in computed tomography and magnetic resonance imaging. The licensing laws covering the practice of these professions vary from state to state. A current list of states that require licensure for radiologic technologists is given in Appendix E. The rules and regulations for licensure change from time to time, so it is best to check with your state board of health. The state might also have a radiologic safety board or similar program that regulates professionals in radiology and related professions.

Nuclear Medicine Technologist

Applicants for admission into a professional training program must have graduated from high school (or its equivalent). Postsecondary competencies in mathematics; science courses such as human anatomy and physiology, physics, and chemistry; and specialized classes in medical terminology and medical ethics are important. Oral and written communications are also emphasized.

The professional portion of the program is one year in length and leads to a certificate. However, the professional training can be integrated into a two-year program leading to an associate degree or a four-year program leading to a bachelor's degree. The curriculum for an accredited program will have classes in patient care, nuclear physics, instrumentation and statistics, health physics, biochemistry, immunology, radiopharmacology, administration, radiation biology, clinical nuclear medicine, radionuclide therapy, and an introduction to computer application.

Upon satisfactory completion of the training program, the applicant can sit for the credentialing examination offered by the Nuclear Medicine Technology Certification Board (NMTCB) or the American Registry of Radiologic Technologists. The NMTCB examination is a timed test (one hour and forty-five minutes) consisting of ninety questions. The examination is task-oriented and deals with the application of basic knowledge to nuclear medical technology practice. Sample examination questions can be found at the NMTCB website at www.nmtcb.org.

If you successfully pass the examination, you are granted the right to use the title Certified Nuclear Medicine Technologist and the initials CNMT after your name. Your name will be listed in the *NMTCB Directory of Certified Nuclear Medicine Technologists*. You are required to renew your certification each year.

The ARRT exam consists of 200 questions in five areas: radiation protection (22 questions), radiopharmaceutical preparation (22), instrumental quality control (28), diagnostic procedures (114), and patient care (14). Individuals with a baccalaureate or associate degree in one of the biological or physical sciences and national certification as a registered medical technologist, registered radiologic technologist, or registered nurse may also request to sit for the certification examination. In addition, they must also have completed eight thousand hours of clinical experience in nuclear medicine technology under the supervision of a physician (M.D./D.O.) who is board certified in nuclear radiology (ABR), nuclear medicine (ABNM), or isotopic pathology (ABP).

Radiologic Technologist (Radiographer)

The applicant for admission for professional training as a radiographer must be a high school graduate (or equivalent), and the high school curriculum described for nuclear medicine technologist would also be appropriate. The typical program is either two or four years in length and is integrated into an associate or baccalaureate degree plan.

The typical curriculum offered at a CAHEA-accredited institution would include introduction to radiography, radiographic procedures, principles of radiographic exposure, imaging equipment, film processing, evaluation of radiographs, radiation physics, principles of radiation protection and radiation biology, and radiographic pathology. It should also include courses on human anatomy and physiology, medical ethics and law, medical terminology, methods of patient care, quality assurance, and computer literacy. A plan for a well-structured, competency-based clinical education, where the student interacts with patients under the supervision of a physician or technologist, is also an important part of the curriculum.

After having satisfactorily completed the training program, the applicant is eligible to sit for the credentialing examination offered by the ARRT. However, candidates for registration must have good moral character. Anyone who is convicted of a felony or any other offense involving moral turpitude will not be permitted to sit for the examination until he or she has served his or her entire sentence (including probation and parole periods) and has had all civil rights restored.

ARRT currently administers eight examinations, with three in the primary radiological sciences: radiography, nuclear medicine technology (described above), and radiation therapy; as well as five advanced-level examinations: cardiovascular-interventional technology, mammography, computer tomography, magnetic resonance imaging, and quality management.

The radiography examination consists of 200 questions in the following areas: radiation protection (30 questions), equipment operation and maintenance (30), image production and evaluation (50), radiographic procedures (60), and patient care (30). Upon satisfactory completion of an accredited training program and passing of the certification examination, the technologist will receive a certificate and pocket credential and have the right to use the title Registered Radiographer. The certificate must be renewed annually. In addition, the technologist has the right to use the abbreviation RT (ARRT) in connection with his or her name on documents, business cards, and name tags. The technologist's name will also appear in the *American Registry of Radiologic Technologists*, which is published every other year.

The radiation therapy exam consists of 200 questions in the following areas: radiation protection and quality assurance (40 questions); treatment planning and delivery (130); and patient care, management, and education (30). The radiation therapy technologist's work centers on utilizing radiation-producing equipment to administer therapeutic doses of radiation to patients, rather than utilizing this equipment for imaging.

Diagnostic Medical Sonographer

A student seeking professional training as a sonographer must be a high school graduate (or equivalent), and the high school curriculum described for nuclear medicine technologist would be appropriate. Professional training programs are either two or four years in length and yield an associate or baccalaureate degree. Some individuals in four-year programs obtain a degree in radiology, with a minor in sonography.

The typical curriculum offered at a CAHEA-accredited institution would include physical sciences, applied biological sciences, patient care, clinical medicine, applications of ultrasound, instrumentation, related diagnostic procedures, and image evaluation. To sit for the credentialing examination offered by the American Registry of Diagnostic Medical Sonographers (ARDMS), graduates of these programs must also have at least one year (thirty-five hours per week for forty-eight weeks) of ultrasound/vascular clinical experience. Graduates of other two-year allied health training programs that focus on patient care, such as radiologic technology, respiratory therapy, occupational therapy, physical therapy, and registered nursing, may also sit for the credentialing examination if they have one year of ultrasound/vascular clinical experience. Physicians (M.D. or D.O.) who are duly licensed to practice medicine in the

United States may also sit for the examination if they have one year of ultrasound/vascular clinical experience. Graduates of two-year nonsonography programs are required to have twenty-four months of clinical experience to sit for the examination. ARDMS also allows individuals who were trained on-the-job to sit for the examination. They must have twenty-four months of clinical experience in ultrasound and an additional twenty-four months of training/experience in an allied health field, such as electrocardiographic or electroencephalographic technology, licensed practical nursing, noninvasive testing, and so forth.

ARDMS offers credentials for the registered diagnostic medical sonographer, the registered diagnostic cardiac sonographer, and the registered vascular technologist. The candidate for registered diagnostic medical sonographer must pass the ultrasound physics and instrumentation examination and a specialty examination in obstetrics and gynecology, abdomen, neurosonology, or ophthalmology. The registered diagnostic cardiac sonographer must pass the cardiovascular principles and instrumentation and physics examinations and either the pediatric or adult echocardiography specialty examination. To become a registered vascular technologist, the candidate must pass the vascular physical principles and instrumentation examination, as well as the vascular technology examination.

The physics/principles examination contains 120 multiple-choice questions and covers the following subjects: elementary principles, propagation of ultrasound through tissues, ultrasound transducers, pulse echo instruments, principles of pulse echo imaging, images, storage and display, Doppler, image features and artifacts, quality assurance of ultrasound instruments, and bioeffects and safety.

The specialty examination is made up of 180 multiple-choice questions and includes a variety of topics. For example, the obstetrics and gynecology specialty examination covers obstetrics (such as first trimester anatomy, second and third trimester anatomy, the placenta, assessment of gestational age, complications, amniotic fluid, genetic studies, fetal demise, fetal abnormalities, and coexisting disorders), gynecology (normal pelvic anatomy, reproductive physiology, infertility/endocrinology, postmenopausal anatomy and physiology, pelvic pathology, and extra-pelvic pathology), and patient care and preparation.

Upon successful completion of the education requirements and passing the examination, ARDMS provides a certificate, identification card, and lapel pin, as well as a listing in the *ARDMS Directory*. ARDMS also publishes a quarterly newsletter, *Registry Reports*.

How to Prepare for a Credentialing Examination

The first step in preparing for the credentialing examinations offered by NMTCB, ARRT, or ARDMS is to understand the appropriate eligibility requirements and be sure that you have met them. Also be sure that the application and supporting paperwork (transcripts, diplomas, and the like) are turned in well before the application deadline.

Read over the application packet so that it is clear what can and cannot be brought into the examination room. Generally, this is limited to several sharpened pencils. Battery-powered calculators are commonly allowed, but sharing calculators is not. It is a good idea to have a wristwatch so that you can pace yourself, as these tests are timed. Typically, you will not be allowed to bring papers, books, dictionaries, or any other material into the examination site. Scratch work is done in the margins of the examination.

The tests are scored on the basis of number of correct answers, so if you do not know an answer, guess! But, make a mark in the margin of the examination and come back to that question if time permits. Each of the credentialing organizations has different methods for attempting to equate the difficulty level of each version of the examination (new versions are used each time the examination is given) and the ability level of the group tested. The procedures are outlined in the application package of each organization.

These examinations are not meant to test basic knowledge, but rather the application of that knowledge to the practice of the profession. Make sure to read over the application package carefully and note what sort of questions are asked in the sample tests, as well as the distribution of questions in specific content areas. And take the practice test. Practice does improve performance!

In the weeks before the examination, review a current textbook in the appropriate area. It is also a good idea to review continuing education articles and teaching editorials in recent journals to provide a review of current clinical practice.

During the week(s) immediately before the examination, be sure to get plenty of rest and eat well—no junk food! Get a good night's rest before the examination.

On the day of the examination, arrive a few minutes early, sit down, close your eyes, and take a few slow, deep breaths. This will help you to relax. If you feel yourself getting nervous during the exam, take a minute to repeat this process.

4

WORKPLACES, RESPONSIBILITIES, AND OPPORTUNITIES FOR ADVANCEMENT

MEDICAL IMAGING TAKES place in a variety of different settings. Because of the cost and size of CT and MRI scanners, this type of imaging tends to occur in hospitals and freestanding imaging centers. A recent poll provides detailed information about the work site of nuclear medical technologists. It is likely that radiologic technologists work in essentially the same settings, although they may be more involved with imaging equipment than with using more traditional X-ray equipment.

Sonography also occurs in these settings, but it is becoming increasingly likely to find sonographic equipment and sonographers in the larger group medical practices, particularly those that deal with obstetrics/gynecology or ophthalmology, as well as those that deal with the cardiovascular system. It is also becoming more likely to find sonography equipment in outpatient clinics, health maintenance organizations, and state or county health departments.

Small Hospitals

Relatively few (about 5 percent) nuclear medical technologists work in small hospitals (1–99 beds). These hospitals are found in small cities and rural communities. Although they may have traditional X-ray equipment, it is unlikely that they would have a CT and especially an MRI scanner. If the hospital has an obstetrics/gynecology department, then it is likely to have sonography equipment.

Medium-Size Hospitals

About a third of all nuclear medical technologists work in medium-size hospitals (100–299 beds). These hospitals are likely to have a variety of imaging equipment, including traditional X-ray equipment, a CT scanner, and potentially an MRI scanner. It is likely that the imaging department will have several sonography machines and that the obstetrics/gynecology department may have its own sonography equipment and dedicated sonographers.

Large Hospitals

About half of all nuclear medicine technologists work in large hospitals (more than 300 beds). Large hospitals, especially large teaching hospitals that are associated with a medical school, are likely to have an X-ray or radiology department, as well as a medical imaging department that has one or more CT scanners and an MRI scanner. Sonography services may be provided by a separate sonography department, or they may be part of the radiology or imaging department. Increasingly obstetrics/gynecology, ophthalmology, and cardiac care services have their own dedicated sonography equipment and sonographers.

Outpatient Imaging Centers

The cost of CT and MRI scanners is prohibitively high at well over $1 million. Improvements in technology occur more rapidly than the useful life cycle of existing equipment. Some health care planners believe that outpatient imaging centers may provide the most economical method of providing CT and MRI services. One outpatient imaging center can serve patients from a number of hospitals, health maintenance organizations, individual physicians, and so on. Currently about 8.5 percent of all nuclear medicine technologists work in this setting.

Educational Institutions

Many of the teachers in CAHEA-accredited programs for nuclear medicine technology, radiologic technology, and sonography are themselves technologists. For example, about 3 percent of all nuclear medicine technologists describe themselves as educators. As shown in Appendixes A, B, and C, these educational programs are found in a variety of institutions, including hospitals, two-year junior or community colleges, or four-year colleges and universities, as well as in a small number of technical schools.

Sales

A small number of technologists (about 2.5 percent) are employed in sales; they sell equipment, supplies, radiopharmaceuticals, and other items. In contrast to the technologists who actually do the imaging, salespeople must generally be willing to travel. Depending on the size of the territory, a salesperson may be away from home overnight to up to several weeks at a time. Salespeople must be very knowledgeable about the equipment and products they sell; they are often called on to train physicians and staff on how to use the equipment or products, demonstrate the equipment or products at medical conferences and trade shows, and troubleshoot equipment when it malfunctions.

Salespeople must be fairly aggressive and possess excellent communication skills. They must also be willing to work independently and thus must be self-starters.

Other Work Sites

Certified nuclear medicine and radiologic technologists receive a good deal of training on radiation safety. Therefore, they can potentially act as radiation health and safety personnel for federal, state, county, or local health and radiation control agencies, as well as industries such as nuclear power plants whose personnel could potentially be exposed to ionizing radiation.

Job Duties and Opportunities for Advancement

It is important to understand that only a medical doctor (M.D.) or a doctor of osteopathic medicine (D.O.) can order either traditional radiologic examinations or CT, MRI, PET, or sonogram scans. Furthermore, only a physician can interpret the results of such a scan. Doctors of chiropractic and podiatry can order and interpret traditional radiologic examinations.

Staff Technologist

This is an entry-level position. The person in this position works in the trenches and has day-to-day contact with patients. Therefore, it is vital that the technologist be a compassionate person who can demonstrate in his or her interactions with a patient that he or she cares about that patient's feelings and concerns. One way to show this is to spend a few minutes with each patient to be sure that the patient understands the procedure. During this time, the technologist can also alleviate any fears the patient may have about the procedure. At all times, the technologist should exhibit a professional demeanor. By actions and speech, the technologist should create the impression of professional competence.

The technologist should have enough information about a patient's medical history so that he or she can perform the ordered diagnostic procedure and maximize its interpretability for the physician who ordered it. The technologist is also responsible for instructing patients before and during the procedure and helping position the patient. This includes being responsible for determining if the procedure was carried out correctly. If the patient moves or if the equipment is not working properly and this results in an uninterpretable scan, the scan should be repeated, so as to save the patient the time and trouble of having to return to the imaging center for a new scan.

Technologists must use their knowledge of radiation physics and safety regulations to minimize radiation exposure to their patients and themselves. In addition, while a patient is under a technologist's care, the technologist must be able to recognize emergency conditions and be able to initiate emergency life-saving first aid when appropriate.

About half of the nuclear medicine technologists at this level indicate that imaging is their main job responsibility. In addition to their duties involving imaging, these technologists must also be able to prepare and administer radiopharmaceuticals. They must be able to use appropriate laboratory equipment to quantify the amount and distribution of radionucleotides in the patient and in specimens obtained from the patient (such as from urine, for example). The technologist must also be prepared to monitor the quality of all procedures and products in the laboratory.

Radiologic technologists have similar duties. In addition to specialized scans such as CT or MRI, these technicians are likely to be involved with using more traditional X-ray equipment. They must be able to use their knowledge of anatomy, physiology, and radiographic technique to correctly instruct the patient about the tests and procedures they perform. These technologists also help position the patients. In addition, they are responsible for processing film and evaluating radiologic equipment.

Sonographers, because of the nature of the sonographic technique, often have more contact with the patient. Sonography equipment is a bit less intimidating than the equipment used in CT or MRI scans, so the patient might be a bit less overwhelmed. The sonographer must be able to perform sonography scans and record anatomical, pathological, and physiological data that will help the physician interpret the results of the scan.

Chief Technologist

The chief technologist, whether he or she is a nuclear medicine or radiologic technologist or a sonographer, supervises staff technologists, students acquiring clinical experience as part of their certification process, laboratory assistants, and other laboratory personnel. Since this position carries more experience, the chief technologist also helps the staff technologists with difficult scans.

Service Director

The service director supervises the chief technologist and other personnel. He or she works in concert with the medical staff and hospital administrators to identify and procure new equipment. The service director will also participate in routine quality control, documenting laboratory operations and helping with any departmental inspections conducted by various licensing, regulatory, and accrediting agencies. The person in this position is also responsible for ordering and maintaining supplies and for scheduling patient examinations.

Radiologist

The medical director of an imaging department is likely to be a radiologist or a physiatrist. A radiologist is a physician who has specialized training in the diagnostic and therapeutic use of X-rays and other forms of radiant energy. A physiatrist is a physician who specializes in physical medicine and uses heat, electricity, and ionizing radiation in the diagnosis and treatment of disease.

5

USING YOUR PEOPLE SKILLS, MANAGING STRESS, AND AVOIDING BURNOUT

WITH THE POSSIBLE exception of a woman who comes to have a routine sonogram during pregnancy, almost all patients (and their family members) who come to an imaging center are under a good deal of stress. As such, they may not be on their best behavior.

The reason that they have come to the imaging center is because someone, usually their family physician or some other medical specialist, suspects (or knows) that they have a serious, potentially life-threatening medical condition. The patient may have just heard frightening words, such as cancer, heart disease, stroke, or internal bleeding.

Or they may be an accident victim or the victim of a violent crime, such as a gunshot or a stabbing. Victims will probably still be shaken by the incident that brought them to the imaging center.

The patient may also be concerned about the cost of the scan. While the physician may consider the results of the scan vital to make a diagnosis and prescribe a treatment, the cost to the patient may not be a trivial consideration. Even with some types of insurance, the patient may have to pay 10 to 40 percent of the cost of the scan. Without insurance, the patient will bear the entire cost.

The equipment in the imaging center can appear forbidding and frightening to someone who is unaccustomed to it. This is especially true of CT and MRI equipment; these machines are large, and patients must actually enter them and remain inside, very still, for a certain amount of time. Patients may feel abandoned because the technologist and family members must leave the immediate area while the scan is being conducted. Infants, young children, and the elderly are more likely to be frightened by the imaging device than would young or middle-aged adults.

Sonographic equipment is smaller, and for most scans the technologist remains with the patient and actually manipulates the transducer to perform the scan.

Medical imaging is a highly technical field, and an imager will learn the technical side of the profession at school. But there is more to medical imaging than its technical aspects. The technologist must always remember that what he or she is imaging is a person. Therefore, in addition to technical skills, the technologist must also possess good people and communication skills. The technologist should be compassionate and have empathy for patients and be able to communicate these feelings to the patients.

People Skills

It is never too early to acquire people skills. The way to acquire people skills is to be around people—as big a cross section of different types of people that you can find—and to interact with them. The process can begin in high school. Take part in extracurricular activities such as clubs, teams, the band, or whatever interests you. Volunteer at a hospital, nursing home, homeless shelter, literacy center, or a crisis hotline. These organizations are always looking for volunteers, and volunteering will bring you into contact with a wide variety of different types of people undergoing a variety of different stresses.

Another way to increase your people skills is by taking classes in the social sciences. Choose this type of class when you are considering electives. Classes dealing with psychology and/or sociology are especially useful. Foreign languages are also helpful. In addition to the language, you acquire some insight into the culture of the people who speak the language.

If you pursue a CAHEA-approved program that leads to an associate or baccalaureate degree, you will probably have electives in these programs, and you can select psychology or sociology courses. You can also continue extracurricular activities and volunteer work. Be sure that these activities do not affect your course work or grades.

Your Own Stresses and Strains

People in the helping professions often have to deal with a lot of unrelieved stress in the workplace. These professions include doctors, nurses, imaging technologists, and other medical or allied medical professionals, just like any other professional group, such as policemen and firemen, who work long and often irregular hours and come into contact with people who are under great stress.

Members of these professions also tend to do shift work. That is, they may work 9:00 A.M. to 5:00 P.M. one week and then midnight to 8:00 A.M. the next week. If there are not enough personnel to cover every shift, some technologists might be asked to work more than one shift. Or they may work eighteen to twenty-four hours on the weekend and then be off for several days.

Members of these professions may also be on call; that is, they must be available to come into work on a moment's notice, such as in the case of an emergency. If the number of technologists at a particular location is small, it may not be possible to rotate on-call duties.

Burnout: How to Recognize It

Burnout can be defined as a debilitating psychological condition brought on by unrelieved stress in the workplace. Although most people who study burnout look at stress in the workplace, students with unresolved stress can also suffer from burnout.

The symptoms of burnout are relatively easy to recognize. Especially in someone else! Generally the first symptom to appear is a depletion of energy reserves. This is characterized by chronic fatigue. You just feel tired all the time. If you have poor eating habits, such as skipping meals, eating junk food or fast food, and/or if you have a poor sleep-wakefulness cycle, these effects can be magnified. If you are on call or if you do shift work, your sleep-wakefulness cycle is likely to be disrupted.

These factors often lead to the second symptom—lowered resistance to illness. When you reach this stage, you will find that you have a lot of minor illnesses, such as colds, sore throats, and so forth. Nothing life threatening, but debilitating, nonetheless.

Individuals who are tired all the time and mildly sick most of the time begin to recognize that something is wrong. At this stage, it is likely that you will experience dissatisfaction and pessimism about your work. If unresolved, this generally leads to an increase in absenteeism and inefficiency. This latter can be a real problem if you are working in a medical setting. If you make a mistake, both you and your patient could suffer from it.

It is easier to be courteous and professional with stressed out patients if you are not stressed out yourself. Remember, it is important to take breaks during the day to catch your breath and recharge. Try to get away from the lab and go somewhere nice for lunch. Utilize days off to do something that you enjoy and that does not have anything to do with work. Try to leave your work at work. When you go home, relax, have something good to eat (junk food is all right occasionally but not as a regular diet), and get plenty of rest. If you have trouble sleeping—a common problem if you are in the beginning stages of burnout—check with a professional. Sleep deprivation can wear you down very quickly.

6

SAFETY

NATURALLY, SAFETY IS of paramount importance in all aspects of medicine. In the course of your day working in the field of medical imaging, you will experience many situations that could pose a hazard not only to your patients, but to you as well. This chapter summarizes some of the more common situations you will encounter and should be prepared to handle.

Patient-Related Safety

When a patient is delivered to the imaging center, his or her immediate care is the responsibility of the center's staff. Therefore, it is vital that you know enough about the patient's condition so that you know what to expect. But also be prepared for the unexpected! You must know what to do if a patient stops breathing, has a convulsion, or has some other minor or major difficulty. You must be sure that you know the rules and regulations of both the imaging center and the institution as a whole with regard to emergencies, and that you are willing and able to implement them.

A patient who is brought to the imaging center will likely be in a wheelchair, on a gurney, or in his or her own bed. While the patient is in your care, be sure that the side rails on the bed or gurney are up or that the patient's seat belt is fastened. This will prevent accidental injuries from falls. If you are performing a CT or MRI scan, it is your responsibility to help the patient move to the patient couch/gantry.

You must evaluate each patient individually. Determine if he or she feels dizzy or weak. If the patient is as big or bigger than you are, it is best to get help. Be sure to wear a back-support belt whenever you move a patient. This will help you to avoid any painful back injuries. Once the patient is on the instrument gantry, you must help position him or her to obtain an optimum image.

Contrast Agents

The purpose of contrast media is to visualize structures or disease processes that would otherwise be invisible with conventional X-rays or CT scans. Barium is used to outline the digestive tract, and iodine in solution is used in most other radio-opaque (impenetrable by radiation) media. Ideally, the radio-opaque medium should be pharmacologically inert; that is, it should not have negative side effects. Unfortunately, this has not been completely achieved. Some patients will experience a feeling of warmth spreading over the body as the medium is injected, and a few will find this objectionable. Concentrated solutions may occasionally cause pain in the upper arm, but raising the arm at the end of the injection can generally alleviate this.

Nausea, vomiting, light-headedness, as well as bronchospasm, laryngeal edema, and hypotension, also occur; however, they are relatively rare. You should know what equipment and drugs are available to treat these conditions. Injection of contrast media outside of a vein can cause pain, so you should be very careful when you perform this procedure.

Patients with known allergic reactions are more likely to have an adverse reaction than nonallergic individuals. Infants, elderly patients, and patients with heart disease, as well as those with renal failure, myeloma, and severe diabetes, are also high-risk groups.

Dealing with Contagious Diseases

Those who work in imaging centers will undoubtedly come into contact with patients who suffer from a variety of contagious diseases. Thus, they must make every effort to protect themselves while still providing optimum care to their patients. Following are some examples of diseases you might have to deal with.

HIV

Until 1981 acquired immune deficiency syndrome (AIDS) was virtually an unknown disease. Unfortunately, the number of infected individuals continues to increase at an alarming rate.

AIDS is caused by the human immunodeficiency virus (HIV) and is spread via contact with infected body fluids, such as semen or blood. If you work in an imaging center located in a large inner-city teaching hospital, it is likely that you will encounter patients with HIV on a daily or even hourly basis. Patients who are bleeding or who might have to be injected with contrast media or a radiopharmaceutical present the most significant risk.

Hepatitis B

Hepatitis B, a viral disease that attacks the liver, is spread by contact with blood and other biological fluids. It is not uniformly fatal like AIDS, but people with hepatitis B are more likely to develop liver cancer or cirrhosis of the liver. It is best to take the same precautions with someone suspected of having hepatitis B as with someone who has AIDS; i.e., wear glove and face protection when giving injections or dealing with situations in which the patient is likely to bleed. There is a vaccine for hepatitis B. Check with a physician to determine whether you should receive it.

Tuberculosis

Since the turn of the last century, the incidence of tuberculosis has been on the decline. This decline was caused by improved public health measures and the development of antibiotics. However, the incidence of tuberculosis is now apparently rising. There are currently a number of strains of the tubercle bacilli that are resistant to commonly used antibiotics, and in some cases they are resistant to combinations of antibiotics. These drug-resistant bacilli developed as a result of patients with tuberculosis not completing their antibiotic treatments. If the antibiotic is stopped before all of the bacilli are killed, the ones that remain are relatively resistant to the antibiotic and rapidly reproduce. Ultimately, the resistant strains are spread to other individuals.

In contrast to AIDS or hepatitis B, tuberculosis can infect the body via a number of different routes, including the digestive and respiratory tract and the conjunctiva (the "third" eyelid in the corner of your eye). Transmission of tuberculosis is airborne and facilitated by close contact. Thus, it is important to wash your hands carefully after handling a patient with tuberculosis and avoid sneezes and coughs that occur in your direction. If you do catch tuberculosis, be sure to complete your antibiotic treatment, so that you do not add to the resistant strains.

The Electromagnetic Spectrum and You

Imaging technology takes advantage of different portions of the electromagnetic spectrum. The electromagnetic spectrum ranges from extremely low frequencies (ELF) such as the sixty-hertz (Hz) fields and potentials in the overhead power lines that provide the electric energy that powers our electric lights, appliances, and computers, as well as imaging equipment. If electromagnetic waves in the ELF-frequency range have any biological impact (there is considerable controversy about this point right now), most investigators believe that the magnetic field would be responsible.

The electromagnetic spectrum extends to radio frequency (about one hundred thousand Hz), microwave frequency (about ten billion Hz) radiation, and visible light (about one hundred trillion Hz).

The effects of electromagnetic radiation in the radio-frequency range (RFR) or microwave-frequency range (MFR) on a living organism are determined by the amount and form of energy that the organism absorbs. In contrast to ELF, if RFR or MFR have some biological impact, it is the electric rather than the magnetic field that is responsible for the effect.

Energy absorption is generally measured in terms of the rate of energy absorption per unit of volume divided by the mass density of the elements in the energy-absorbing object; this is generally expressed in watts per kilogram (W/kg). It is generally agreed that significant effects do not occur until energy absorption reaches one

W/kg, and hazardous effects do not occur until energy absorption reaches four W/kg. These effects are due primarily to increases in body temperature caused by the absorbed energy.

Ultraviolet rays (about one quadrillion Hz) are responsible for the sunburn you receive if you spend too much time in the sunlight. Ultraviolet waves form the upper edge of visible light (some organisms, such as honeybees, can apparently see ultraviolet waves), and they possess enough energy (more than ten electron volts) to ionize atoms. Shorter wavelengths, such as X-rays or delta rays, possess considerably more energy (more than one million electron volts).

Sonogram Scanners

High-resolution sonographic transducers that are used to resolve small objects, such as parts of the eye, emit frequencies in the 10.0-MHz range. Sonographic transducers used to scan larger structures, such as the abdomen, emit frequencies that are in the range of 2.5 MHz. Their wavelengths are relatively long (from 0.01 to 100.0 meters) and their energies relatively small (about 0.000001 electron volt). Since diagnostic ultrasound intensities range from one to ten milliwatts per square centimeter, it is very unlikely that they would deposit enough energy to cause a significant change in the temperature of the tissue or organ under investigation. Small increases in local temperature will occur as a result of relaxation processes and molecular friction or agitation, caused by the movement of molecules as the sound wave passes through matter. There have been no reports of immediate or late effects that have occurred in humans exposed to diagnostic levels of medical ultrasound. The absolute minimum dose to cause significant biological effects in animal models is one hundred milliwatts per square centimeter, at least ten times more powerful than the dose typically used in diagnostic ultrasound, and effects only occurred after many hours of continuous exposure.

Radionuclide Imaging

Radioactive isotopes are used in diagnostic imaging because they release gamma rays as they decay—that is, they naturally lose their radioactivity. Gamma rays are similar to X-rays, but they occur as a result of decay of the nucleus. To minimize the radiation dose to the patient, imagers use the smallest possible dose of an isotope with a short half-life. (The half-life of an isotope is the period of time required for a quantity of radioactivity to be reduced to one half of its original value.) The radionuclide technetium-99m is commonly used for thyroid and vascular imaging. It has a half-life of six hours and emits gamma radiation at a suitable energy that allows for easy detection. Technetium-99m can be attached to other molecules that concentrate selectively in different parts of the body. For example, if technetium-99m is tagged with a complex organic phosphate, it will be taken up and concentrated by the bones, thus allowing the skeleton to be visualized.

The gamma rays that are emitted by the isotope as it decays are detected by a gamma camera, which consists of a sodium iodide crystal that is attached to a number of photo-multiplier tubes. When a gamma ray strikes the sodium iodide crystal, it causes the crystal to emit a photon of light. The light is electrically amplified and converted to an electrical pulse by the photo-multiplier tube. The output of the tube is attached to a computer that allows further manipulation and enhancement of the signal. If the gamma camera moves around the patient, the process is called single photon emission computed tomography.

CT Scans

The CT scan allows very small differences in X-ray absorption to be visualized. The range of densities of a typical X-ray film produced by conventional radiology is about twenty, but the range of densities in a CT scan of the same structures is about two thousand.

Images produced through CT scans are often distorted by the presence of radiating linear streaks. These streaks make it harder to look at surrounding structures. They are generally caused by movement of the patient (remember, the exposure is typically one to two seconds long) or by objects with very high density.

Ionizing radiation from X-rays or gamma rays is potentially harmful, especially to dividing cells. Unnecessary exposure to X-rays or gamma rays should be avoided, especially since their effects tend to be cumulative.

The World Health Organization—Basic Radiological System Advisory Group recommends that you always do the following:

- Stand behind the control panel when an X-ray exposure is made.
- Wear lead aprons and lead gloves if a patient needs to be held.
- Do not allow anyone to remain in the room with the patient.
- Always wear your film badge or other dosimeter (radiation-measuring device), and have it checked regularly.
- Never perform any scan unless a physician orders it.

Remember, X-rays can harm you even though you cannot see or feel them; however, X-rays are only dangerous if you are careless.

Film badges were introduced in the mid-1940s. They consist of a small piece of radiographic film sandwiched between two metal (usually aluminum or copper) filters inside a plastic holder. Film badges should be worn with their proper side to the front. Film badges should not be worn for more than one month, since heat and humidity will alter their sensitivity. Film badges are sensitive to exposures of less than twenty megaroentgens.

Thermoluminescent dosimeters contain lithium fluoride in crystal form. These dosimeters cost about twice as much as film dosimeters, but they are more sensitive (over five megaroentgens) and can be worn for as long as three months. If the lithium fluoride is exposed to radiation, the crystal absorbs the energy and stores it in the form of excited electrons in the crystal. If the crystal is heated, the excited electrons fall back to their normal state, which causes the emission of visible light. The intensity of the light, as measured by a photo-multiplier tube, is proportional to the radiation dose to which the crystal was exposed.

Pocket ionization chambers are generally two centimeters in diameter and ten centimeters long and are clipped to clothing like a writing pen. This dosimeter must be charged to a predetermined voltage. When the dosimeter is exposed to radiation, the charge is dissipated and neutralized. The typical range of the dosimeter is up to two hundred milliroentgens. If exposure exceeds this range, the precise level of exposure might be difficult to determine.

MRI Scans

MRI scans can be directly reconstructed in any plane. MRI scans are relatively slow when compared to CT scans (several minutes as opposed to a few seconds). The patient must remain still for this time. Unavoidable movements such as breathing tend to degrade the image. MRI does not require a source of ionizing radiation. But all MRI imagers have strong static magnetic fields. The Bureau of Radiologic Health (BRH), the federal agency responsible for establishing safety standards, recommends an upper limit of two tesla, because harmful biological or genetic effects have not been observed below this level. Static magnetic fields well above this level (such as twenty-four tesla) can cause changes in the electric activity of nerves and the heart.

On the other hand, ferromagnetic objects (objects that make a good magnet) can be potentially dangerous to you and your patient when the static field is turned on. No metallic object should be allowed in the MRI room unless it is carefully checked to determine its response to strong magnetic fields. Electronic metal detectors, much like those used at airports, can be used to detect metal objects on or in the patient or any accompanying persons. Unfortunately, metal detectors are not sensitive to small objects, so there is no substitute for a careful and detailed history of the patient and a careful inspection of the patient with a magnet to detect such small metal objects. Fortunately, most surgically implanted stainless steel devices (like aneurysm clips and prostheses) are relatively nonmagnetic.

Cardiac pacemakers may be adversely affected. The switch that permits external control of common pacemakers is magnetically controlled. Also, ferromagnetic components of the pacemaker may be attracted by the field and cause the pacemaker to reposition it.

MRI scanners also produce alternating magnetic fields, which can induce electric currents in the patient's tissues and in metallic objects within or next to the patient. The BRH recommends the upper limits for such magnetic fields to be three tesla per second.

MRI scanners also produce radio-frequency radiation that ranges in frequency from one to one hundred MHz. RFR can cause heating of the tissue, due to induced electric currents, as well as atomic and molecular oscillations. The quantity of current produced is proportional to the square of the RFR frequency and is also proportional to the square of the diameter of the subject. Superficial tissues will typically receive the greatest amount of heat. Human studies have reported that the temperature increase is about one degree Celsius, which is within the normal daily variation in temperature. When the alternating magnetic field is turned on, a relatively loud sound (sixty-five to ninety-five decibels) is produced.

Medium-high and high MRI scanners use superconducting magnets. These superconducting magnets require cryogens (liquid helium or nitrogen) to cool them to allow them to develop superconductivity. These liquid and gaseous elements are extremely dangerous. They are very cold and can cause frostbite. Cryogen spills or quenching of the magnet can release large amounts of cryogen gases that can replace oxygen and asphyxiate those in the immediate vicinity.

It is not currently clear what impact, if any, the static and alternating magnetic fields might have on a pregnant female or her fetus. The Food and Drug Administration has not given approval for routine MRI scans of pregnant females.

Radiation Sickness

Most experts agree that radiation exposure should not exceed five thousand milliroentgens annually. The lethal dose that within thirty days can kill 50 percent of the individuals exposed to it (commonly called the LD50/30 dose) is a single exposure of about 300 rads if no postexposure supportive treatment is provided, and about 850 rads if postexposure treatment is provided. If you know and follow standard safety standards, your exposure should never come close to this amount.

Acute radiation-induced death in humans is unlikely to occur in an imaging setting because the X-rays and gamma rays are neither sufficiently intense nor large enough to cause death. Some accidental exposures in the nuclear weapon or nuclear energy fields have occurred. The acute radiation syndrome occurs following high-level, whole-body exposure to radiation and consists of three syndromes: hematologic, gastrointestinal, and neuromuscular. Which of these three syndromes occurs depends on the dose of radiation.

With all three syndromes there is an initial phase that consists of clinical symptoms that occur within hours of high-level radiation exposure and continue for one or two days. This is followed by a latent period that can last hours to weeks. During the latent phase, there is no clinical sign of radiation sickness. The latent phase is followed by a period of manifest radiation sickness.

The initial phases of the hematologic syndrome include nausea, vomiting, diarrhea, and a decrease of white blood cells in the blood. Following the latent phase, the manifest illness of the hematologic syndrome is characterized by a continued reduction in the numbers of white and red cells, as well as platelets. If the radiation dose was sufficiently high, the reduction in blood cells will continue unchecked until the body's defenses against infections and other disorders is nil. If the radiation dose is not lethal, recovery can begin within two to four weeks of exposure and may take as long as six months.

If the radiation dose is higher, the gastrointestinal syndrome will follow the latent period. This is characterized by a second wave of vomiting and diarrhea, as well as a loss of appetite and lethargy. The diarrhea will increase in severity and will lead to loose, then watery, and then bloody stools. Death usually occurs as a result of severe damage to the cells lining the intestines.

If the radiation dose is extremely high, the neuromuscular syndrome occurs. The initial phase of this syndrome is characterized by severe vomiting and nausea. The person will also be extremely nervous and confused and will complain of loss of vision and a burning sensation on the skin. This is followed by a latent period of six to twelve hours, during which the symptoms will decrease in intensity or disappear. After the latent period, the initial symptoms will reappear, but with greater intensity. They will be accompanied by disorientation and loss of muscle coordination. The person may have difficulty breathing and may have one or more convulsions. Ultimately, he or she will become lethargic, lapse into a coma, and die. The principal causes of death are an elevated fluid content in the brain, changes in the blood vessels in the brain, and inflammation of the meninges.

Remember safety first! Think before you act. Do not allow yourself to engage in shortcuts to save a few seconds, because any variance from well-thought-out procedures can lead to problems. One of the simplest ways to avoid infections is to eat well, get plenty of rest, and wash your hands regularly.

Appendix A

Accredited Nuclear Medicine Technology Programs

Alabama

University of Alabama at
Birmingham
Nuclear Medicine Technology
Program
1705 University Blvd.
Birmingham, AL 35294-1212
www.uab.edu/nmtprogram

Arkansas

Baptist Health
School of Nuclear Medicine
Technology
11900 Colonel Glenn Rd.,
Ste. 1000
Little Rock, AR 72210-2820
www.baptist-health.org

University of Arkansas for
Medical Sciences
College of Health Related
Professions
4301 W. Markham St., #714
Little Rock, AR 72205
www.uams.edu/chrp/nuc_med
.htm

California

Charles R. Drew University of
Medicine & Science
Nuclear Medicine Technology
Program
1731 E. 120th St.,
KECK Bldg.
Los Angeles, CA 90059
www.cdrewu.edu

VA Palo Alto Health Care
  System
Nuclear Medicine
  Technologist Training
  Program
3801 Miranda Ave.
Palo Alto, CA 94304
www.palo-alto-med.va.gov

Kaiser Permanente School of
  Allied Health Sciences
Nuclear Medicine Program
938 Marina Way S.
Richmond, CA 94804
http://kpsahs.kp.org

South Coast Nuclear
  Medicine
Santa Barbara Nuclear
  Medicine
Technologist Training
  Program
229 Pueblo St.
Santa Barbara, CA 93105
www.nmtcb.org/schools.shtml

Harbor-UCLA Medical
  Center
Division of Nuclear Medicine
1000 W. Carson St., Box 23
Torrance, CA 90509
www.harbor-ucla.org

Connecticut

Gateway Community College
Nuclear Medicine Technology
  Program
88 Bassett Rd.
New Haven, CT 06473
www.gwctc.commnet.edu

Delaware

Delaware Technical and
  Community College
Nuclear Medicine Technology
  Program
333 Shipley St.
Wilmington, DE 19801
www.dtec.edu/wilmington/
  ah/nmt.html

Florida

Broward Community College
Nuclear Medicine Technology
  Program
Center for Health Science
  Education, Bldg. 41-137
1000 Coconut Creek Blvd.
Coconut Creek, FL 33066
www.broward.edu

Santa Fe Community College
Nuclear Medicine Technology
  Program
3000 NW 83rd St.
Gainesville, FL 32606-6200
www.santafe.cc.fl.us

St. Vincent's Medical Center
School of Nuclear Medicine
1800 Barrs St.
Jacksonville, FL 32204
www.jaxhealth.com

Jackson Memorial Hospital
Program in Nuclear Medicine
  Technology
1611 NW 12th Ave., C-250
Miami, FL 33136

Florida Hospital College of
  Health Sciences
Nuclear Medicine Technology
  Program
711 Lake Estelle Dr.
Orlando, FL 32803
www.fhchs.edu

Hillsborough Community
  College
Nuclear Medicine Technology
  Program
P.O. Box 30030
Tampa, FL 33630
www.hccfl.edu

Georgia

Medical College of Georgia,
  SAHS
Department of Radiologic
  Sciences AE-2003
Nuclear Medicine Technology
  Program
1120 15th St.
Augusta, GA 30912-0600
www.mcg.edu/radscape/
  nuclearmedicine/index.htm

Middle Georgia Technical
  College
School of Nuclear Medicine
  Technology
80 Cohen Walker Dr.
Warner Robins, GA 31088
www.mgtc.org

Illinois

Northwestern Memorial
  Hospital
School of Nuclear Medicine
  Technology
Galter, 8th Fl.
251 E. Huron St.
Chicago, IL 60611-2908
www.nmh.org/nmh/forhealth
  careprofessionals/sdnmt
  .htm

College of Du Page
Nuclear Medicine Technology
    Program
425 Fawell Blvd.
Glen Ellyn, IL 60137-6599
www.cod.edu

Edward Hines Jr. VA Hospital
School of Nuclear Medicine
    Technology
Nuclear Medicine Service
    (115F)
Fifth Ave. & Roosevelt Rd.
Hines, IL 60141-5000
www.visn12.med.va.gov/
    hines/abo/

Triton College
Nuclear Medicine Technology
    Program
2000 N. Fifth Ave.
River Grove, IL 60171-1995
www.triton.cc.il.us

Indiana

Indiana University School of
    Medicine
Nuclear Medicine Technology
    Program
541 Clinical Dr., CL 120
Indianapolis, IN 46202-5111
www.indyrad.iupui.edu

Iowa

University of Iowa Hospitals
    & Clinics
Nuclear Medicine Technology
    Program 3834 JPP
Department of Radiology
    Nuclear Medical
200 Hawkins Dr.
Iowa City, IA 52242-1009
www.uihealthcare.com/ui
    hospitalsandclinics

Kansas

University of Kansas Medical
    Center
Program of Nuclear Medicine
3901 Rainbow Blvd., Mail
    Stop 4032
Kansas City, KS 66160-7234
www.rad.kumc.edu/nucmed

Kentucky

Jefferson Community College
Nuclear Medicine Technology
    Program
109 E. Broadway
Louisville, KY 40202-2005
www.jcc.kctcs.edu

Louisiana

Delgado Community College
Nuclear Medicine Technology
  Program
Allied Health Division
615 City Park Ave.
New Orleans, LA 70119
www.dcc.edu

Maine

Central Maine Medical Center
School of Nuclear Medical
  Technology
300 Main St.
Lewiston, ME 04240-0305
www.cmmc.org

Maryland

The Johns Hopkins Hospital
School of Medical Imaging
  and Nuclear Medicine
  Technology Program
8 Market Pl., Ste. 600
Baltimore, MD 21202
www.hopkinsmedicine.org

Prince George's Community
  College
Allied Health Department
Nuclear Medicine Technology
  Program
301 Largo Rd.
Largo, MD 20772-2199
http://pgweb.pg.cc.md.us

Massachusetts

Massachusetts College of
  Pharmacy & Health
  Science
Nuclear Medicine Technology
  Program
179 Longwood Ave.
Boston, MA 02215
www.mcphs.edu

Salem State College
Nuclear Medicine Technology
  Program
Biology Dept.
352 Lafayette St.
Salem, MA 01970-5353
www.salemstate.edu

Springfield Technical
Community College
Nuclear Medicine Technology
Program
1 Armory Square
P.O. Box 9000
Springfield, MA 01105-9000
www.stcc.edu

University of Massachusetts
Medical Center
Worcester State College
Nuclear Medicine Technology
Program
55 Lake Ave. N.
Worcester, MA 01665
www.worcester.edu

Michigan

Ferris State University
Nuclear Medicine Technology
Program
College of Allied Health
Sciences
200 Ferris Dr., VFS 411
Big Rapids, MI 49307-9989
www.ferris.edu

William Beaumont Hospital
Nuclear Medicine Technology
Program
3601 W. 13 Mile Rd.
Royal Oak, MI 48073-6769
www.beaumonthospitals.com

Minnesota

Mayo School of Health
Sciences
NMT Program
200 SW First St.
Rochester, MN 55905
www.mayo.edu/mshs

St. Mary's University of
Minnesota
Nuclear Medicine Technology
Program
700 Terrace Heights, #10
Winona, MN 55987-1399
www.smumn.edu

Mississippi

University of Mississippi
Medical Center
Nuclear Medicine Technology
Program
2500 N. State St.
Jackson, MS 39216-4505
www.umc.edu

Missouri

University of
Missouri–Columbia
Nuclear Medicine Technology
Program
605 Lewis Hall
Columbia, MO 65211-0001
www.missouri.edu

Research Medical Center
School of Nuclear Medicine
Technology
2316 E. Meyer Blvd.
Kansas City, MO 64132
www.researchmedical
center.com

St. Louis University
Nuclear Medicine Technology
Program
School of Allied Health
Professions
3437 Caroline St.
St. Louis, MO 63104-1395
www.slu.edu

Nebraska

University of Nebraska
Medical Center
Nuclear Medicine Technology
Program
School of Allied Health
Professions
981045 Nebraska Medical
Center
Omaha, NE 68198-1045
www.unmc.edu

Nevada

University of Nevada
Nuclear Medicine Technology
Program
4505 S. Maryland Pkwy.
Las Vegas, NV 89154-3017
www.unlv.edu

New Jersey

Muhlenberg Regional Medical
Center
School of Nuclear Medicine
Technology
Park Ave. and Randolph Rd.
Plainfield, NJ 07061
www.muhlenbergschools.org

University of Medicine &
Dentistry of New Jersey
School of Health Related
Professions
Nuclear Medicine Technology
Program
1776 Raritan Rd., Rm. 538
Scotch Plains, NJ 07076
www.umdnj.edu

Gloucester County College
Nuclear Medicine Technology
Program
1400 Tanyard Rd.
Sewell, NJ 08080
www.gccnj.edu

New York

Bronx Community College
Nuclear Medicine Technology
Program
University Ave. &
W. 181st St.
Bronx, NY 10453
www.bcc.cuny.edu

University at Buffalo–SUNY
Nuclear Medicine Technology
Program
105 Parker Hall
3435 Main St.
Buffalo, NY 14214-3007
www.nucmed.buffalo.edu/nmt

Institute of Allied Medical
Professions
Nuclear Medicine Technology
Program
405 Park Ave., Ste. 501
New York, NY 10022-4405
www.iampedu.com

St. Vincent's Hospital &
Medical Center
Nuclear Medicine Technology
Program
153 W. 11th St.
New York, NY 10011
www.nucmedicine.com

Northport Department of VA
Medical Center
School of Nuclear Medicine
Technology
79 Middleville Rd.
Northport, NY 11768-2290
www1.va.gov/visns/visn03/
nrptinfo.asp

Rochester Institute of
  Technology
Nuclear Medicine Technology
  Program
Department of Allied Health
  Sciences
85 Lomb Memorial Dr.,
  P.O. Box 9887
Rochester, NY 14623-5603
www.rit.edu

Molloy College
Nuclear Medicine Technology
  Program
1000 Hempstead Ave.
P.O. Box 5002
Rockville Centre, NY 11571
www.molloy.edu

North Carolina

University of North Carolina
  Hospitals
Nuclear Medicine Technology
  Program
Department of Radiology
CB#7510, 101 Manning Dr.
Chapel Hill, NC 27599
www.med.unc.edu/radiology

Caldwell Community College
  & Technical Institute
Nuclear Medicine Technology
  Program
2855 Hickory Blvd.
Hudson, NC 28638-2397
www.caldwell.cc.nc.us

Forsyth Technical
  Community College
Nuclear Medicine Technology
  Program
2100 Silas Creek Pkwy.
Winston-Salem, NC 27103
www.caldwell.cc.nc.us/health
  sci/nuclear_mt_main.htm

Ohio

Aultman Hospital
Nuclear Medicine Technology
  Program
2600 6th St. SW
Canton, OH 44710-1799
www.aultman.com

University of Cincinnati
Advanced Medical Imaging
  Technology Program
202 Goodman Ave.
Cincinnati, OH 45267
www.cahs.uc.edu/depart
  ments/amit.cfm

Ohio State University Medical
  Center
School of Nuclear Medicine
  Technology
410 W. 10th Ave.
Columbus, OH 43210-1228
http://amp.osu.edu/rd

The University of Findlay
Nuclear Medicine Institute
1000 N. Main St.
Findlay, OH 45840-3695
www.findlay.edu

Cuyahoga Community
  College
Nuclear Medicine Technology
  Program
11000 Pleasant Valley Rd.
Western Campus
Parma, OH 44130
www.tri-c.edu/nmed

Kent State University
Radiologic & Imaging
  Sciences
Nuclear Medicine Technology
  Program
2491 State Route 45 South
Salem, OH 44460
www.salem.kent.edu/academic
  programs/rismainmenu.cfm

St. Elizabeth Health Center
School of Nuclear Medicine
  Technology Program
1044 Belmont Ave.
Youngstown, OH 44501

Oklahoma

University of Oklahoma at
  Oklahoma City
Health Science Center
Department of Radiologic
  Technology
P.O. Box 26901, CHS-451
Oklahoma City, OK 73190
www.ah.ouhsc.edu/radtech

Pennsylvania

Cedar Crest College
Nuclear Medicine Technology
  Program
100 College Dr.
Allentown, PA 18104-6196
www2.cedarcrest.edu/academ
  ic/bio/nmt/nmt.htm

Lancaster General College of
  Nursing & Health Science
School of Nuclear Medical
  Technology
Lancaster General Hospital
410 N. Lime St.
Lancaster, PA 17602-3555
www.lancastergeneral.org/con
  tent/nuclear_medicine.asp

Jameson Health System
School of Nuclear Medicine
  Technology
South Campus
1100 S. Mercer St.
New Castle, PA 16101
www.jamesonhealthsystem
  .com

Community College of
  Allegheny County
Nuclear Medicine Technology
  Program
808 Ridge Ave.
Pittsburgh, PA 15212-6097
www.ccac.edu/default.aspx?id=
  138729

Wyoming Valley Health Care
  System
School of Nuclear Medical
  Technology
575 N. River St.
Wilkes Barre, PA 18764
wvhcs.org/hospitals/school
  _nuclear_med.html

Abington Memorial Hospital
School of Nuclear Medicine
2500 Maryland Rd., Ste. 211
Willow Grove, PA 19090
www.amh.org/education/radio
  logictech.htm

Puerto Rico

University of Puerto Rico
Nuclear Medicine Technology
  Program
College of Health Related
  Professions
Medicine Sciences Campus
P.O. Box 365067
San Juan, PR 00936-5067
www.rcm.upr.edu

Rhode Island

Rhode Island Hospital
School of Nuclear Medicine
Technology
Learning Center of Diagnostic
Imaging
3 Davol Sq., Bldg. A, 4th Fl.
Providence, RI 02903
www.lifespan.org/diagimag/
nuclear/default.htm

South Carolina

Midlands Technical College
School of Nuclear Medicine
Technology
P.O. Box 2408
Columbia, SC 29202
www.midlandstech.edu/
nucmed

South Dakota

Southeast Technical Institute
Nuclear Medicine Technology
Program
2320 N. Career Ave.
Sioux Falls, SD 57107
www.southeasttech.com

Tennessee

Chattanooga State Technical
Community College
Nuclear Medicine Technology
Program
Business, Industry & Health
Bldg., Ste. 107
4501 Amnicola Hwy.
Chattanooga, TN 37406
www.chattanoogastate.edu/
allied_health/nuclear.asp

University of Tennessee
Medical Center–Knoxville
School of Nuclear Medicine
Technology
1924 Alcoa Hwy.
Knoxville, TN 37920-6999
www.utmedicalcenter.org

Baptist College of Health
Sciences
Nuclear Medicine Technology
Program
1003 Monroe
Memphis, TN 38104
www.bchs.edu

Methodist Healthcare School
of Radiologic and Imaging
Sciences
Nuclear Medicine Technology
Program
1265 Union Ave.
Memphis, TN 38104
www.methodisthealth.org

Vanderbilt University Medical
Center
Nuclear Medicine Technology
Program
1161 21st Ave.
South Room CCC-1124
MCN
Nashville, TN 37232-2675
www.mc.vanderbilt.edu/
radiology/education/
nmtechnology.php

Texas

Amarillo College
Nuclear Medicine Technology
Program
P.O. Box 447
Amarillo, TX 79178
http://sites.actx.edu/~nuclear
_med

Baylor University Medical
Center
Radiology Allied Health
School, NMT Program
3500 Gaston Ave.
Dallas, TX 75246
www.baylorhealth.edu/rahs

Galveston College
Nuclear Medicine Technology
Program
4015 Ave. Q
Galveston, TX 77550-2782
www.gc.edu/gc/nuclear
_medicine_technology_aas
.asp?snid=1286900032

Houston Community College
System
Nuclear Medicine Technology
Program
MC 1637-H519
1900 Galen Dr.
Houston, TX 77030
http://hccs.edu/discipline/
nmtt/nmttabot.html

University of the Incarnate
  Word
Nuclear Medicine Science
4301 Broadway
San Antonio, TX 78209-6397
www.uiw.edu/snhp/nukemed
  .html

Utah

University of Utah Health
  Sciences Center
Nuclear Medicine Division
50 N. Medical Dr.
Salt Lake City, UT 84132
www.uuhsc.utah.edu/rad/nuc
  med/nmt.html

Vermont

University of Vermont
Nuclear Medicine Technology
  Program
Biomedical Technologies
  Dept.
Rowell Bldg., Rm. 302
Burlington, VT 05405
www.uvm.edu

Virginia

Old Dominion University
Program in Nuclear Medicine
  Technology
School of Medical Laboratory
  Sciences
Environmental Health
209 Spong Hall
Norfolk, VA 23529-0287
www.odu.edu/hs/cohs/nmed/
  index.html

Naval School of Health
  Sciences
Nuclear Medicine
  Technologist Program
1001 Holcomb Rd.
Portsmouth, VA 23708-5200
http://nshs.med.navy.mil

Virginia Commonwealth
  University
Nuclear Medicine Technology
  Program
701 W. Grace St.
Richmond, VA 23298-3057
www.vcu.edu/nucmed

Washington

Bellevue Community College
Nuclear Medicine Technology
 Program
3000 Landerholm Circle SE
Bellevue, WA 98007-6484
www.bcc.ctc.edu/nucmed

West Virginia

West Virginia State College
Community & Technical
 College
Nuclear Medicine Technology
 Program
P.O. Box 1000, Campus
 Box 183
Institute, WV 25112-1000
www.wvsc.edu

West Virginia University
 Hospital
School of Nuclear Medicine
 Radiologic Technology
Medical Center Dr.,
P.O. Box 8062
Morgantown, WV 26505
www.wvuh.radtech.com

Wheeling Jesuit University
Nuclear Medicine Technology
 Program
316 Washington Ave.
Wheeling, WV 26003-6295
www.wju.edu/academics/nme/
 facts.asp

Wisconsin

Gundersen Lutheran Medical
 Foundation
Nuclear Medicine Technology
 Program
1836 South Ave.
LaCrosse, WI 54601
www.gundluth.org

St. Joseph's Hospital
School of Nuclear Medicine
 Technology
611 St. Joseph Ave.
Marshfield, WI 54449
www.ministryhealth.org/
 display/ppf/docid/192/
 router.aspx

Froedtert Memorial Lutheran
Hospital
Nuclear Medicine Technology
Program
9200 W. Wisconsin Ave.
Milwaukee, WI 53226-3596
www.froedtert.com

St. Luke's Medical Center
Nuclear Medicine Technology
Program
2900 W. Oklahoma Ave.
Milwaukee, WI 53215-2901
www.aurorahealthcare.org

Appendix B

Accredited Radiologic Technologist (Radiographer) Programs

Alabama

Carraway Methodist Medical
   Center
1600 Carraway Blvd.
Birmingham, AL 35234
www.carraway.org

Jefferson State Community
   College
2601 Carson Rd.
Birmingham, AL 35215-3098
www.jeffstateonline.com

University of Alabama
1705 University Blvd., RMSB
   447
Birmingham, AL 35294-1270
http://main.uab.edu/show.asp?
   durki=3417

George C. Wallace
   Community College
1141 Wallace Dr.
Dothan, AL 36303
www.wallace.edu

Gadsden State Community
   College
1001 Wallace Dr.
P.O. Box 227
Gadsden, AL 35902-0227
www.gadsdenst.cc.al.us

Wallace State Community
   College
P.O. Box 2000
Hanceville, AL 35077-2000
www.wallacestate.edu

Huntsville Hospital
101 Sivley Rd.
Huntsville, AL 35801
www.hhsys.org/radschool/rad
_school.php

University of South Alabama
1504 Springhill Ave.
Mobile, AL 36604-3273
www.southalabama.edu

Baptist Medical Center South
2169 Normandie Dr.
Montgomery, AL 36111
www.baptistfirst.org

Southern Union State
Community College
1701 Lafayette Pkwy.
Opelika, AL 36801
www.suscc.edu

DCH Regional Medical
Center
809 University Blvd. E.
Tuscaloosa, AL 35401
www.dchsystem.com

Arizona

Pima Medical Institute
957 S. Dobson Rd.
Mesa, AZ 85202
www.pmi.edu

Apollo College–Phoenix
U.S. Education Corporation
2701 W. Bethany Home Rd.
Phoenix, AZ 85017
www.apollocollege.edu

GateWay Community College
108 N. 40th St.
Phoenix, AZ 85034
www.gwc.maricopa.edu

Pima County Community
College
2202 W. Anklam Rd.
HRP 220
Tucson, AZ 85709-0080
http://wc.pima.edu

Pima Medical Institute
3350 E. Grant Rd.
Tucson, AZ 85716
www.pmi.edu

Arkansas

South Arkansas Community
College
P.O. Box 7010
300 S. West Ave.
El Dorado, AR 71731-7010
www.southark.edu

University of Arkansas for
   Medical Sciences
AHEC-Northwest
2907 E. Joyce Blvd.
Fayetteville, AR 72703
www.uams.edu/ahec/ahec12
   .htm

University of
   Arkansas–Fort Smith
5201 Grand Ave.
P.O. Box 3649
Fort Smith, AR 72913-3649
www.uafortsmith.edu

North Arkansas College
1515 Pioneer Dr.
Harrison, AR 72601
www.northark.edu

National Park Community
   College
101 College Dr.
Hot Springs, AR 71913-9174
www.npcc.edu

Baptist Health Medical
   Center–Little Rock
11900 Colonel Glenn Rd.
Little Rock, AR 72210-2820

Central Arkansas Radiation
   Therapy Institute
P.O. Box 55050
Little Rock, AR 72215
www.carti.com

St. Vincent Infirmary Medical
   Center
2 St. Vincent Circle
Little Rock, AR 72205-5499
www.stvincenthealth.com

University of Arkansas for
   Medical Sciences
4301 W. Markham, Slot 563
Little Rock, AR 72205
www.uams.edu/chrp/rad-tech

Southeast Arkansas College
1900 South Hazel St.
Pine Bluff, AR 71603
www.seark.edu

Arkansas State University
P.O. Box 910
State University, AR 72467
www.clt.astate.edu/radsci

University of Arkansas for
   Medical Sciences
300 E. 6 St.
Texarkana, AR 71854
www.uams.edu

California

Cabrillo College
6500 Soquel Dr.
Aptos, CA 95003
www.cabrillo.edu

Bakersfield College
1801 Panorama Dr.
Bakersfield, CA 93305
www.bakersfieldcollege.edu

Mills-Peninsula Health
    Services
1783 El Camino Real
Burlingame, CA 94010
www.millspeninsula.org

Pima Medical Institute
780 Bay Blvd., Ste. 101
Chula Vista, CA 91910
www.pimamedical.com

Arrowhead Regional Medical
    Center
400 N. Pepper Ave.
Colton, CA 92324-1819
www.co.san-bernardino.ca.us/
    armc

Orange Coast College
2701 Fairview Rd.
P.O. Box 5005
Costa Mesa, CA 92628-5005
www.orangecoastcollege.edu

Cypress College
9200 Valley View St.
Cypress, CA 90630-5897
www.cypresscollege.edu

City of Hope National
    Medical Center
1500 East Duarte Rd.
Duarte, CA 91010
www.cityofhope.org/rad
    therapy

Fresno City College
1101 E. University Ave.
Fresno, CA 93741
www.fresnocitycollege.com

Loma Linda University
School of Allied Health
    Professions
Loma Linda, CA 92350
www.llu.edu/sahp

California State
    University–Long Beach
1250 Bellflower Blvd.
Long Beach, CA 90840-4902
www.csulb.edu

Foothill College
12345 El Monte Rd.
Los Altos Hills, CA 94022-
    4599
www.foothill.fhda.edu

Charles R. Drew University of
  Medicine & Science
1731 E. 120th St.
Los Angeles, CA 90059-3025
www.cdrewu.edu

Los Angeles City College
855 N. Vermont Ave.
Los Angeles, CA 90029
www.lacitycollege.edu

Yuba Community College
2088 N. Beale Rd.
Marysville, CA 95901
www.yccd.edu

Merced College
3600 M St., Box #7
Merced, CA 95348-2898
www.mccd.edu/alliedhealth/
  radtechhp.htm

Moorpark College
7075 Campus Rd.
Moorpark, CA 93021
www.moorparkcollege.edu

California State
  University–Northridge
18111 Nordhoff St.
Northridge, CA 91330-8285
www.csun.edu

Merritt College
12500 Campus Dr.
Oakland, CA 94619
www.merritt.edu

Pasadena City College
1570 E. Colorado Blvd.
Pasadena, CA 91106-2003
www.pasadena.edu

Chaffey College
5885 Haven Ave.
Rancho Cucamonga, CA
  91737-3002
www.chaffey.edu

Canada College
4200 Farm Hill Blvd.
Redwood City, CA 94061
www.canadacollege.net

Kaiser Permanente Medical
  Center–Richmond
938 Marina Way S.
Richmond, CA 94804-3739
www.kpsahs.org

Naval School of Health
  Sciences
34101 Farenholt Ave.
San Diego, CA 92134-5291
http://nshssd.med.navy.mil

San Diego Mesa College
7250 Mesa College Dr.
San Diego, CA 92111
www.sdmesa.sdccd.cc.ca.us

City College of San Francisco
50 Phelan Ave., Box S91
San Francisco, CA 94112
www.ccsf.edu

Central California School of
   Continuing Education
3195 McMillan, #F
San Luis Obispo, CA 93401
www.ccsce.org

Santa Barbara City College
721 Cliff Dr.
Santa Barbara, CA 93109-
   2394
www.sbcc.net

Santa Rosa Junior College
1501 Mendocino Ave.
Santa Rosa, CA 95401-4395
www.santarosa.edu

San Joaquin General Hospital
P.O. Box 1020
Stockton, CA 95201
www.sjgeneralhospital.com

El Camino College
16007 S. Crenshaw Blvd.
Torrance, CA 90506
www.elcamino.edu/radiologic
   technology

L.A. County Harbor/UCLA
   Medical Center
1000 W. Carson St., Box 27
Torrance, CA 90509-2910
www.humc.edu

Mount San Antonio College
1100 N. Grand Ave.
Walnut, CA 91789-1399
www.mtsac.edu

Colorado

Red Rocks Community
   College
5420 Miller St., #7181
Arvada, CO 80002-3069
www.rrcc.edu

ConCorde Career Institute
111 N. Havana St.
Aurora, CO 80010
www.concorde.edu

Memorial Hospital
175 S. Union Blvd., Ste. 240
Colorado Springs, CO 80910
www.memorialhospital.com/
radschool

Community College of
Denver
1070 Alton Way
Denver, CO 80230
www.ccd.rightchoice.org

Pima Medical Institute
1701 W. 72nd Ave., Ste. 130
Denver, CO 80221
www.pima.edu

St. Anthony Hospitals,
Centura Health
1601 N. Lowell Blvd.
Denver, CO 80204-1597
www.stanthonycentral.org

Mesa State College
1100 North Ave.
Grand Junction, CO 81501
www.mesastate.edu

Aims Community College
5401 W. 20th St.
P.O. Box 69
Greeley, CO 80632
www.aims.edu

Connecticut

St. Vincent's College
2800 Main St.
Bridgeport, CT 06606
www.stvincentscollege.edu

Danbury Hospital
24 Hospital Ave.
Danbury, CT 06810
www.danburyhospital.org

Quinnipiac University
275 Mount Carmel Ave.
Hamden, CT 06518
www.quinnipiac.edu

Capital Community Technical
College
950 Main St.
Hartford, CT 06103
www.ccc.commnet.edu

Hartford Hospital
560 Hudson St.
Hartford, CT 06106
www.harthosp.org

Middlesex Community
College
100 Training Hill Rd.
Middletown, CT 06457
www.radiologyschool.com

Gateway Community
   Technical College
88 Bassett Rd.
North Haven, CT 06473
www.gwcc.commnet.edu

Stamford Hospital
Box 9317
Stamford, CT 06904-9317
www.stamhealth.org

Naugatuck Valley Community
   College
750 Chase Pkwy.
Waterbury, CT 06708
www.nvctc.commnet.edu

University of Hartford
200 Bloomfield Ave.
West Hartford, CT 06117
www.hartford.edu

Windham Community
   Memorial Hospital
112 Mansfield Ave.
Willimantic, CT 06226
www.windhamhospital.org

Delaware

Delaware Technical &
   Community College
School of Radiography
P.O. Box 610
Southern Campus
Georgetown, DE 19947
www.dtcc.edu

Delaware Technical &
   Community College
School of Radiography
333 Shipley St.
Wilmington, DE 19801
www.dtcc.edu

District of Columbia

Howard University
Sixth & Bryant St. SW
Washington, DC 20059
www.howard.edu

University of the District of
   Columbia
Department of Nursing and
   Allied Health NW
4200 Connecticut Ave.
Washington, DC 20008
www.udc.edu

Washington Hospital Center
110 Irving St. NW
Washington, DC 20010
www.whcenter.org

Florida

MedVance Institute–Atlantis
KIMC Investments, Inc.
5503 S. Congress Ave., Ste.
203
Atlantis, FL 33467
www.medvance.org

West Boca Medical Center
21644 State Rd. 7
Boca Raton, FL 33428
www.gc.edu

Bethesda Memorial Hospital,
Inc.
2815 S. Seacrest Blvd.
Boynton Beach, FL 33435
www.bethesdaweb.com/bmh
.shtml

Manatee Community College
5840 26th St. W.
P.O. Box 1849
Bradenton, FL 34206-1849
www.mccfl.edu

Radiation Therapy School for
Radiation Therapy
Technology, Inc.
1419 SE 8th Terr.
Cape Coral, FL 33990
www.21stcenturyoncology
.com/school

Brevard Community College
1519 Clearlake Rd.
Cocoa, FL 32922
www.brevardcc.edu

Halifax Medical Center
303 N. Clyde Morris Blvd.
Daytona Beach, FL 32114
www.hfch.org/hmc

Keiser College–Daytona
Beach
1800 Business Park Blvd.
Daytona Beach, FL 32114
www.keisercollege.edu

Keiser College–Ft. Lauderdale
1500 NW 49th St.
Ft. Lauderdale, FL 33309
www.keisercollege.edu

Edison Community College
8099 College Pkwy. SW
P.O. Box 60210
Fort Myers, FL 33906-6210
www.edison.edu

Indian River Community
  College
3209 Virginia Ave.
Fort Pierce, FL 34981-5599
www.ircc.edu

Santa Fe Community College
3000 NW 83rd St.
Gainesville, FL 32606-6200
www.santafe.cc.fl.us

St. Vincent's Medical Center
1800 Barrs St.
P.O. Box 2982
Jacksonville, FL 32204
www.jaxhealth.com

SHANDS Jacksonville School
  of Radiologic Technology
655 W. 8th St.
Jacksonville, FL 32209
www.shandsjacksonville.org/
  schools/rad

Lakeland Regional Medical
  Center
P.O. Box 95448
Lakeland, FL 33804
www.lrmc.com

University of Miami
Jackson Memorial Hospital
  Medical Center
1611 NW 12th Ave.
Miami, FL 33136-1094
www.um-jmh.org

Miami Dade College
Medical Center Campus
950 NW 20th St.
Miami, FL 33127
www.mdc.edu

Professional Training Centers
13926 SW 47th St.
Miami, FL 33175
www.ptcmatt.com

Marion County School of
  Radiologic Technology
1014 SW 7th Rd.
Ocala, FL 34474
www.mcctae.com

Florida Hospital College of
  Health Sciences
800 Lake Estelle Dr.
Orlando, FL 32803
www.fhchs.edu

University of Central Florida
4000 Central Florida Blvd.
HPA II, Rm. 210K
Orlando, FL 32816-2220
www.cohpa.ucf.edu

Valencia Community College
P.O. Box 3028
Mail Code 4-14
Orlando, FL 32802-3028
www.valenciacc.edu

Palm Beach Community
  College
3160 PGA Blvd.
Palm Beach Gardens, FL
  33410-2893
www.pbcc.edu/radiography/
  index.asp

Gulf Coast Community
  College
5230 W. US Hwy. 98
Panama City, FL 32401-1041
www.gulfcoast.edu

Pensacola Junior College
5555 W. Hwy. 98
Pensacola, FL 32507-1097
www.pjc.edu

MedVance Institute–
  Ft. Lauderdale
KIMC Investments, Inc.
4101 S. Hospital Dr., Ste. 9
Plantation, FL 33317
www.medvance.org.

Keiser College–Sarasota
  Campus
6151 Lake Osprey Dr.
Sarasota, FL 34240
www.keisercollege.edu

Hillsborough Community
  College
4001 Tampa Bay Blvd.
Tampa, FL 33614
www.hccfl.edu

Polk Community College
999 Ave. H NW
Winter Haven, FL 33881
www.polk.edu

Georgia

Albany Technical Institute
1704 S. Slappey Blvd.
Albany, GA 31701
www.albanytech.edu

Athens Technical College
800 US Hwy. 29 N.
Athens, GA 30601-1500
www.athenstech.edu

Atlanta Medical Center
303 Parkway Dr. NE, Box 51
Atlanta, GA 30312-1206

Emory University School of
    Medicine
1364 Clifton Rd. NE,
    Rm. BG07
Atlanta, GA 30322
www.radiology.emory.edu/rad
    tech

Grady Memorial Hospital
Grady Health System
80 Jesse Hill Jr. Dr. SE
Box 26095
Atlanta, GA 30303-3050
www.gradyhealthsystem.org

North Metro Technical
    College
2000 S. Park Pl.
Atlanta, GA 30339
www.northmetrotech.edu

Medical College of Georgia
821 St. Sebastian Way
Augusta, GA 30912
www.mcg.edu

University Hospital
1350 Walton Way
Augusta, GA 30901-3599

Coastal Georgia Community
    College
3700 Altama Ave.
Brunswick, GA 31520-3644
www.cgcc.edu

Columbus Technical College
928 Manchester Expressway
Columbus, GA 31904-6572
www.columbustech.edu

Dalton State College
213 N. College Dr.
Dalton, GA 30720
www.daltonstate.edu

DeKalb Medical Center
2701 N. Decatur Rd.
Decatur, GA 30033
www.dekalbmedicalcenter.org

West Central Technical
   College
4600 Timber Ridge Dr.
Douglasville, GA 30135
www.westcentraltech.edu

Heart of Georgia Technical
   College
560 Pinehill Rd.
Dublin, GA 31021-8896
www.hgtc.org

Griffin Technical College
501 Varsity Rd.
Griffin, GA 30223-2042
www.griffintech.edu

West Georgia Technical
   College
303 Fort Dr.
LaGrange, GA 30240
www.westgatech.edu

Gwinnett Technical College
5150 Sugarloaf Pkwy.
Lawrenceville, GA 30043
www.gwinnetttech.edu

Moultrie Technical College
361 Industrial Dr.
Moultrie, GA 31768
www.moultrietech.edu

Coosa Valley Technical
   College
1 Maurice Culberson Dr.
Rome, GA 30161
www.coosavalleytech.edu

Armstrong Atlantic State
   University
11935 Abercorn St.
Savannah, GA 31419-1997
www.radsci.armstrong.edu

Ogeechee Technical College
1 Joe Kennedy Blvd.
Statesboro, GA 30458
www.ogeecheetech.edu

Valdosta Technical Institute
P.O. Box 928, Val-Tech Rd.
Valdosta, GA 31603
www.valdostatetech.edu

Southeastern Technical
   College
3001 E. First St.
Vidalia, GA 30474
www.southeasterntech.edu

Middle Georgia Technical
   College
80 Cohen Walker Dr.
Warner Robins, GA 31088
www.middlegatech.edu

Okefenokee Technical College
1701 Carswell Ave.
Waycross, GA 31503
www.okefenokeetech.edu

Hawaii

University of Hawaii
Kapiolani Community College
4303 Diamond Head Rd.
Honolulu, HI 96816
www.kcc.hawaii.edu

Idaho

Boise State University
1910 University Dr.
Boise, ID 83725
http://radsci.boisestate.edu

College of Southern Idaho
315 Falls Ave.
Twin Falls, ID 83303-1238
www.csi.edu

Illinois

Southwestern Illinois College
2500 Carlyle Ave.
Belleville, IL 62221-9989
www.swic.edu

Southern Illinois
University–Carbondale
College of Applied Science &
Arts, Office 18
Carbondale, IL 62901
www.siuc.edu

Kaskaskia College
27210 College Rd.
Centralia, IL 62801
www.kaskaskia.edu

Parkland College
2400 W. Bradley Ave.
Champaign, IL 61821-1899
www.parkland.cc.il.us

Advocate Illinois Masonic
Medical Center
836 W. Wellington Ave.
Chicago, IL 60657
www.advocatehealth.com

Advocate Trinity Hospital
2320 E. 93rd St.
Chicago, IL 60617
www.advocatehealth.com

Malcolm X Community
College
1900 W. Van Buren St.
Chicago, IL 60612
www.malcolmx.ccc.edu

Northwestern Memorial
   Hospital
251 E. Huron St.
Galter Pavillion LC-178
Chicago, IL 60611
www.nmh.org

Wilbur Wright College
4300 N. Narragansett Ave.
Chicago, IL 60634
www.wright.ccc.edu

Danville Area Community
   College
200 E. Main St.
Danville, IL 61832
www.dacc.cc.il.us

Sauk Valley College
173 Illinois, Rt. #2
Dixon, IL 61021-9112
www.svcc.edu

St. Francis Hospital
355 Ridge Ave.
Evanston, IL 60202
www.reshealth.org

Carl Sandburg College
2400 Tom L. Wilson Blvd.
Galesburg, IL 61401
www.sandburg.edu

College of DuPage
425 Fawell Blvd.
Glen Ellyn, IL 60137
www.cod.edu

College of Lake County
19351 W. Washington St.
Grayslake, IL 60030-1198
www.clcillinois.edu

McDonough District Hospital
525 E. Grant St.
Macomb, IL 61455
www.mdh.org

Kishwaukee College
21193 Malta Rd.
Malta, IL 60150-9699
www.kishwaukeecollege.edu

Bloomington-Normal School
   of Radiography
Bromenn Regional Medical
   Center
900 Franklin Ave.
Normal, IL 61761-4604
www.bnradiography.com

Olney Central College
305 N. West St.
Olney, IL 62450
www.iecc.cc.il.us/occ

Moraine Valley Community
College
10900 S. 88th Ave.
Palos Hills, IL 60465
www.morainevalley.edu/health
sciences

Illinois Central College
Thomas K. Thomas Bldg.
201 SW Adams St.
Peoria, IL 61635-0001
www.icc.edu/haps/radiography

OSF St. Francis Medical
Center
530 NE Glen Oak Ave.
Peoria, IL 61637
www.osfsaintfrancis.org

Blessing Hospital
1005 Broadway
Quincy, IL 62301-7005
www.blessinghospital.org

Triton College
2000 N. Fifth Ave.
River Grove, IL 60171
www.triton.edu

Trinity College of Nursing
and Health Sciences
2122 25th Ave.
Rock Island, IL 61201
www.trinitycollegeqc.edu

Rockford Memorial Hospital
2400 N. Rockton Ave.
Rockford, IL 61101

Swedish-American Hospital
1401 E. State St.
Rockford, IL 61104-2315
www.swedishamerican.org

South Suburban College
15800 S. State St.
South Holland, IL 60473
www.ssc.cc.il.us

Lincoln Land Community
College
5250 Shepherd Rd.
P.O. Box 19256
Springfield, IL 62794-9256
www.llcc.edu

Indiana

Columbus Regional Hospital
2400 E. 17th St.
Columbus, IN 47201
www.crh.org

University of Southern
Indiana
8600 University Blvd.
Evansville, IN 47712
www.usi.edu

Fort Wayne School of
  Radiography
700 Broadway Ave.
Fort Wayne, IN 46802
www.ipfw.edu/radiography

University of St. Francis
2701 Spring St.
Fort Wayne, IN 46808
www.sf.edu

Indiana University Northwest
Division of Nursing & Health
  Professions
3400 Broadway
Gary, IN 46408-1197
www.iun.edu/~ahealth/
  radiation.htm

Hancock Memorial Hospital
  and Health Services
801 N. State St.
Greenfield, IN 46140
www.hmnhs.org

Ball State University
College of Sciences and
  Humanities
Department of Physiology
  and Health Sciences
Indianapolis, IN 47306-0510
www.bsu.edu/physiology
  -health

Community Health Network
School of Radiologic
  Technology
1500 N. Ritter Ave.
Indianapolis, IN 46219
www.ecommunity.com/
  radiologyschool

Indiana University School of
  Medicine
Department of Radiation
  Oncology
Ball Residence, Rm. 112
1226 W. Michigan St.
Indianapolis, IN 46202-5180
www.medicine.iu.edu

Indiana University School of
  Medicine
Department of Radiology
541 Clinical Dr., CL 120
Indianapolis, IN 46202-5111
www.medicine.iu.edu

Ivy Tech State
  College–Indianapolis
P.O. Box 1763
Indianapolis, IN 46206-1763
www.ivytech.edu/indianapolis

St. Joseph Hospital
2001 W. 86th St.
Indianapolis, IN 46240
www.stjosephhospital.net

Indiana University Kokomo
2300 S. Washington St.
Kokomo, IN 46902
www.iuk.edu

King's Daughters' Hospital
and Health Services
1 King's Daughters' Dr.
P.O. Box 447
Madison, IN 47250
www.kingsdaughtershospital
.org

Ivy Tech State
College–Marion
1015 E. 3rd St.
Marion, IN 46952
www.ivytech.edu

Ball Memorial Hospital
2401 University Ave.
Muncie, IN 47303-3499
www.cardinalhealthsystem
.org/radschool.html

Ball State University
College of Sciences and
Humanities
Dept. of Physiology and
Health Sciences
Muncie, IN 47306
www.bsu.edu

Reid Hospital and Health
Care Services
1401 Chester Blvd.
Richmond, IN 47374
www.reidhosp.com

Indiana University
1700 Mishawaka Ave.
P.O. Box 7111
South Bend, IN 46634-7111
www.iusb.edu/-radahlt

Ivy Tech State College
7999 US Hwy. 41 S.
Terre Haute, IN 47802-4898
http://ivytech7.cc.in.us

Porter-Valparaiso Hospital
Campus
814 La Porte Ave.
Valparaiso, IN 46383
www.porterhealth.org

Good Samaritan Hospital
520 S. 7th St.
Vincennes, IN 47591

Iowa

Scott Community College
500 Belmont Rd.
Bettendorf, IA 52722-5649
www.eicc.edu/scc/radiology/
index.html

Mercy/St. Luke's Hospitals
P.O. Box 3026
Cedar Rapids, IA 52402-3026

Jennie Edmundson Memorial
  Hospital
933 E. Pierce St.
Council Bluffs, IA 51503

Iowa Methodist Medical
  Center
1200 Pleasant St.
Des Moines, IA 50309-1453

Mercy College of Health
  Sciences
928 6th Ave.
Des Moines, IA 50309
www.mchs.edu

Iowa Central Community
  College
Fort Dodge Center
330 Ave. M
Fort Dodge, IA 50501
www.iccc.cc.ia.us

University of Iowa Hospitals
  and Clinics
200 Hawkins Dr., C-723
  GG-Radiology
Iowa City, IA 52242-1077
www.radiology.uiowa.edu/
  radtech

Mercy Medical Center–North
  Iowa
1000 4th St. SW
Mason City, IA 50401
www.mercynorth iowa.com

Indian Hills Community
  College
525 Grandview, Bldg. 6
Ottumwa, IA 52501
www.ihcc.cc.ia.us

Northeast Iowa Community
  College
Peosta Campus
10250 Sundown Rd.
Peosta, IA 52068
www.nicc.edu

St. Luke's College
2720 Stone Park Blvd.
Sioux City, IA 51104
www.stlukescollege.org

Allen College
1825 Logan Ave.
Waterloo, IA 50703
www.allencollege.edu

Covenant Medical Center
3421 W. 9th St.
Waterloo, IA 50702
www.covhealth.com

Kansas

Fort Hays State University
600 Park St.
Hays, KS 67601-4099
www.fhsu.edu

Hutchinson Community
  College
815 N. Walnut, Davis Hall
Hutchinson, KS 67501
www.hutchcc.edu

Labette Community College
200 S. 14th St.
Parsons, KS 67357
www.labette.edu

Washburn University–Topeka
1700 SW College Ave.
Topeka, KS 66621
www.washburn.edu

Newman University
3100 McCormick Ave.
Wichita, KS 67213-2097
www.newmanu.edu

Kentucky

King's Daughters' Medical
  Center
2201 Lexington Ave.
Ashland, KY 41101
www.kdmc.com

Bowling Green Technical
  College
1845 Loop Dr.
Bowling Green, KY 42101
www.bowlinggreen.kctcs.edu

Elizabethtown Community
  and Technical College
620 College St. Rd.
Elizabethtown, KY 42701
www.elizabethtown.kctcs.edu

Hazard/Southeast Community
  College
1 Community College Dr.
Hazard, KY 41701

Northern Kentucky University
227 Albright Health Center
Highland Heights, KY 41099
www.nku.edu

Central Kentucky Technical
  College
308 Vo-Tech Rd.
Lexington, KY 40511-1020
www.central.kctcs.edu

St. Joseph Healthcare
West Campus/St. Joseph
  Healthcare
1 St. Joseph Dr.
Lexington, KY 40504
www.sjhlex.org

University of Kentucky
Chandler Medical Center
800 Rose St., Rm. N-13
Lexington, KY 40536-0293
www.uky.edu

James Graham Brown Cancer
   Center
University of Louisville
   Hospital
529 S. Jackson St.
Louisville, KY 40202
www.browncancercenter.org

Jefferson Community &
   Technical College
109 East Broadway
Louisville, KY 40202
www.jcc.kctcs.edu

Spencerian College
4627 Dixie Hwy.
Louisville, KY 40216
www.spencerian.edu

Madisonville Community
   College
750 N. Laffoon St.
Madisonville, KY 42431
www.madcc.kctcs.edu

Morehead State University
150 University Blvd.
Reed Hall 408
Morehead, KY 40351
www.morehead-st.edu

Owensboro Community and
   Technical College
4800 New Hartford Rd.
Owensboro, KY 42303
www.octc.kctcs.edu

West Kentucky Community
   and Technical College
P.O. Box 7380
Paducah, KY 42002-7380
www.westkentucky.kctcs.edu

Southeast Kentucky
   Community and Technical
   College
3300 S. Hwy. 25 E.
Pineville, KY 40977
www.southeast.kctcs.edu

Somerset Community College
808 Monticello St.
Somerset, KY 42501
www.somcc.kctcs.edu

Louisiana

Baton Rouge General Medical
  Center
3600 Florida Blvd.
Baton Rouge, LA 70806
www.brgeneral.org

MedVance Institute of Baton
  Rouge
9255 Interline Ave.
Baton Rouge, LA 70809
www.medvance.org

Our Lady of the Lake College
7434 Perkins Rd.
Baton Rouge, LA 70808
www.ololcollege.edu

Louisiana State University at
  Eunice
P.O. Box 1129
Eunice, LA 70535
www.lsue.edu

North Oaks Medical Center
P.O. Box 2668
Hammond, LA 70404
www.northoaks.org

Lafayette General Medical
  Center
P.O. Box 52009
Lafayette, LA 70505

University Medical Center
LSU Medical Center Service
  Division
2390 W. Congress
P.O. Box 69300
Lafayette, LA 70596-9300

McNeese State University
P.O. Box 92000
Lake Charles, LA 70609
www.mcneese.edu

University of Louisiana
  Monroe
700 University Ave.
Monroe, LA 71209-0450
www.ulm.edu/radtech

Delgado Community College
615 City Park Ave.
New Orleans, LA 70119
www.dcc.edu

Our Lady of Holy Cross
  College
Ochsner Clinic Foundation
1516 Jefferson Hwy.
New Orleans, LA 70121
www.olhcc.edu

Northwestern State University
1800 Line Ave.
Shreveport, LA 71101-4653
www.nsula.edu

Southern University at
Shreveport
3050 Martin Luther King
Jr. Dr.
Shreveport, LA 71107
www.susla.edu

Maine

Eastern Maine Community
College
354 Hogan Rd.
Bangor, ME 04401
www.emcc.edu

Central Maine Medical Center
300 Main St.
Lewiston, ME 04240-0305
www.cmmc.org

Mercy Hospital
144 State St.
Portland, ME 04101
www.mercyhospital.com

Southern Maine Community
College
2 Fort Rd.
South Portland, ME 04106
www.smccme.edu

Maryland

Anne Arundel Community
College
101 College Pkwy.
Arnold, MD 21012-1895
www.aacc.edu

Community College of
Baltimore County
Essex Campus
7201 Rossville Blvd.
Baltimore, MD 21237-9987
www.ccbcmd.edu

Greater Baltimore Medical
Center
6701 N. Charles St.
Baltimore, MD 21204
www.gbmc.org

The Johns Hopkins Hospital
Schools of Medical Imaging
600 N. Wolfe St.,
Blalock B-179
Baltimore, MD 21287
http://radiologycareers.rad
.jhmi.edu

Maryland General Hospital
827 Linden Ave.
Baltimore, MD 21201
www.marylandgeneral.org

Allegany College of Maryland
12401 Willowbrook Rd. SE
Cumberland, MD 21502
www.allegany.edu

Hagerstown Community
  College
11400 Robinwood Dr.
Hagerstown, MD 21742
www.hcc.cc.md.us

Prince George's Community
  College
301 Largo Rd.
Largo, MD 20774-2199
www.pgcc.edu

Wor-Wic Community College
32000 Campus Dr.
Salisbury, MD 21804
www.worwic.edu

Holy Cross Hospital
1500 Forest Glen Rd.
Silver Spring, MD 20910
www.holycrosshealth.org

Montgomery College
7600 Takoma Ave.
Takoma Park, MD 20912
www.montgomerycollege.edu

Washington Adventist
  Hospital
7600 Carroll Ave.
Takoma Park, MD 20912
www.adventisthealthcare.com

Chesapeake College
P.O. Box 8
Wye Mills, MD 21679
www.chesapeake.edu

Massachusetts

Middlesex Community
  College
591 Springs Rd.
Bedford, MA 01730-1197
www.middlesex.cc.ma.us

Bunker Hill Community
  College
250 New Rutherford Ave.
Boston, MA 02129-2925
www.bhcc.mass.edu

Laboure College
2120 Dorchester Ave.
Boston, MA 02124-5698
www.laboure.edu

Massachusetts College of
Pharmacy and Health
Sciences
179 Longwood Ave.
Boston, MA 02115-5896
www.mcphs.edu

Suffolk University
Physics Department
41 Temple St.
Boston, MA 02114
www.suffolk.edu/cas/medical
sciences

Massasoit Community
College
1 Massasoit Blvd.
Brockton, MA 02302
www.massasoit.mass.edu

North Shore Community
College
1 Ferncroft Rd.
P.O. Box 3340
Danvers, MA 01923-0840
www.northshore.edu

MassBay Community College
19 Flagg Dr.
Framingham, MA 01702
www.massbay.edu

Holyoke Community College
303 Homestead Ave.
Holyoke, MA 01040
www.hcc.mass.edu

Northern Essex Community
College
Lawrence Campus
45 Franklin St.
Lawrence, MA 01830-2399
www.necc.mass.edu

Springfield Technical
Community College
1 Armory Sq., Box 9000
Springfield, MA 01102-9000
www.stcc.edu

Quinsigamond Community
College
670 W. Boylston St.
Worcester, MA 01606-2092
www.qcc.mass.edu/
radiography

UMass Memorial Medical
Center
55 Lake Ave. N.
Worcester, MA 01655
www.umassmemorial.org

Michigan

Washtenaw Community
   College
4800 E. Huron River Dr.
Ann Arbor, MI 48106-0978
www.wccnet.edu

Kellogg Community College
450 North Ave.
Battle Creek, MI 49017-3397
www.kellogg.edu

Lake Michigan College
2755 E. Napier Ave.
Benton Harbor, MI 49022
www.lakemichigancollege.edu

Ferris State University
901 S. State St.
Big Rapids, MI 49307-9989
www.ferris.edu

Henry Ford Community
   College
Health Careers Division
5101 Evergreen Rd.
Dearborn, MI 48128-1495
www.hfcc.edu

Henry Ford Hospital
2799 W. Grand Blvd.
Detroit, MI 48202
www.henryfordhealth.org

St. John Hospital and Medical
   Center
22101 Moross Rd.
Detroit, MI 48236-2172
www.stjohn.org

Sinai-Grace Hospital
6071 W. Outer Dr.
Detroit, MI 48235
www.sinai-grace.org

Wayne State University
Department of Radiation
   Oncology
1st Level UHC DMC
Detroit, MI 48201
www.bulletins.wayne.edu

Hurley Medical Center
1 Hurley Plaza
Flint, MI 48503
www.hurleymc.com/education

University of Michigan–Flint
303 E. Kearsley St.
Flint, MI 48502-1950
www.flint.umich.edu/
   departments

Grand Rapids Community
   College
143 Bostwick NE
Grand Rapids, MI 49503
www.grcc.edu

Grand Valley State University
301 Michigan St. NE, Ste.
   200
Grand Rapids, MI 49503
www.gvsu.edu

Mid-Michigan Community
   College
1375 S. Clare Ave.
Harrison, MI 48625-9447
www.midmich.edu

Baker College of Jackson
2800 Springport Rd.
Jackson, MI 49202
www.baker.edu

Lansing Community College
Dept. 3100
P.O. Box 40010
Lansing, MI 48901-7210
www.lansing.cc.mi.us

Marquette General Health
   System
420 W. Magnetic St.
Marquette, MI 49855
www.mgh.org

Baker College–Owosso
1020 S. Washington St.
Owosso, MI 48867-4400
www.baker.edu

Port Huron Hospital
1221 Pine Grove Ave.
Port Huron, MI 48060
www.porthuronhosp.org

William Beaumont Hospital
3601 W. 13-Mile Rd.
Royal Oak, MI 48073-6769
www.beaumont.edu/allied
   health

Oakland Community College
22322 Rutland Dr.
Southfield, MI 48075-4793
www.oaklandcc.edu

Providence Hospital and
   Medical Centers
16001 W. Nine Mile Rd.
Southfield, MI 48037
www.providence-hospital.org

Delta College
1961 Delta Dr.
University Center, MI 48710
www.delta.edu

Minnesota

Riverland Community
   College
1900 8th Ave. NW
Austin, MN 55912
www.riverland.edu

Lake Superior College
2101 Trinity Rd.
Duluth, MN 55811-2741
www.lsc.mnscu.edu

Argosy University–Twin Cities
1515 Central Parkway
Eagan, MN 55121
www.argosyu.edu

Northland Community and
Technical College
2022 Central Ave. NE
East Grand Forks, MN
56721-2702
www.northlandcollege.edu

College of St. Catherine–
Minneapolis
601 25th Ave. S.
Minneapolis, MN 55454
www.stkate.edu

Fairview-University Medical
Center
420 Delaware St. SE
Mayo Mail Code 292
Minneapolis, MN 55455
www.fairview-university
.fairview.org

Veterans Affairs Medical
Center
1 Veterans Dr., #114
Minneapolis, MN 55417
www.visn23.med.va.gov/
service-areas/minneapolis
-vamc.asp

North Memorial Medical
Center
3300 Oakdale Ave. N.
Robbinsdale, MN 55422
www.northmemorial.com

Mayo School of Health
Sciences
Mayo Clinic College of
Medicine
200 First St. SW
Rochester, MN 55905
www.mayo.edu/mshs

St. Cloud Hospital
1406 6th Ave. N.
St. Cloud, MN 56303

Methodist Hospital
6500 Excelsior Blvd.
St. Louis Park, MN 55426

Century College
3300 Century Ave. N.
White Bear Lake, MN 55110
www.century.mnscu.edu

Rice Memorial Hospital
301 Becker Ave. SW
Willmar, MN 56201-3302
www.ricehospital.com

Mississippi

Northeast Mississippi
Community College
101 Cunningham Blvd.
Booneville, MS 38829
www.necc.cc.ms.us

Jones County Junior College
900 Court St.
Ellisville, MS 39437
www.jcjc.edu

Itawamba Community
College
602 W. Hill St.
Fulton, MS 38843-0999
www.iccms.edu

Mississippi Gulf Coast
Community College
Jackson County Campus
P.O. Box 100
Gautier, MS 39553
www.mgccc.cc.ms.us

Pearl River Community
College
5448 US Hwy. 49 S.
Hattiesburg, MS 39401
www.prcc.edu

University of Mississippi
Medical Center
2500 N. State St.
Jackson, MS 39216-4505
http://radtech.umc.edu

Meridian Community College
910 Hwy. 19 N.
Meridian, MS 39307-5890
www.meridiancc.edu

Mississippi Delta Community
College
P.O. Box 668
Moorhead, MS 38761
www.msdelta.edu

Hinds Community College
PMB 10458
Raymond, MS 39154-9799
www.hindscc.edu

Copiah-Lincoln Community
College
P.O. Box 649
Wesson, MS 39191
www.colin.edu

Missouri

Southeast Missouri Hospital
College of Nursing and
    Health Sciences
2001 William St., 2nd Fl.
Cape Girardeau, MO 63703
www.sehcollege.org

University of Missouri
605 Lewis Hall
Columbia, MO 65211
www.hsc.missouri.edu

Mineral Area Regional
    Medical Center
1212 Weber Rd.
Farmington, MO 63640-3398
www.marmc.org

Sanford-Brown College
1203 Smizer Mill Rd.
Fenton, MO 63026
www.sanfordbrown.edu

Nichols Career Center
609 Union
Jefferson City, MO 65101
www.jcps.k12.mo.us

Missouri Southern State
    College
3950 Newman Rd.
Joplin, MO 64801-1595
www.mssu.edu

Avila College
11901 Wornall Rd.
Kansas City, MO 64145
www.avila.edu

Colorado Technical University
520 E. 19th St.
Kansas City, MO 64116
www.coloradotech.edu

Penn Valley Community
    College
3201 SW Trafficway
Kansas City, MO 64111

Research Medical Center
2316 E. Meyer Blvd.
Kansas City, MO 64132-1199
www.researchmedicalcenter
    .com

St. Luke's Hospital of Kansas
    City
4401 Wornall Rd.
Kansas City, MO 64111
www.saint-lukes.org

Rolla Technical Center
500 Forum Dr.
Rolla, MO 65401

State Fair Community College
3201 W. 16th St.
Sedalia, MO 65301
http://sfcc.cc.mo.us

Cox Health School of
   Radiation Therapy
3850 S. National Ave.,
   Ste. 100
Springfield, MO 65807
www.coxhealth.com/schools
   education/radiation
   therapy/default.htm

Cox Health School of
   Radiologic Technology
3801 S. National Ave.
Springfield, MO 65807-5297
www.coxhealth.com

St. John's Regional Health
   Center
1235 E. Cherokee St.
Springfield, MO 65804-2263
www.stjohns.net

Hillyard Technical Center
3434 Faraon St.
St. Joseph, MO 64506
www.hillyardtech.com

Barnes-Jewish College of
   Nursing and Allied Health
306 S. Kings Hwy. Blvd.
St. Louis, MO 63110-1090
www.jhconah.edu

St. John's Mercy Medical
   Center
615 S. New Ballas Rd.
St. Louis, MO 63141
www.stjohnsmercy.org

St. Louis Community College
   at Forest Park
5600 Oakland Ave.
St. Louis, MO 63110
www.stlcc.cc.mo.us/fp

Montana

Benefis Healthcare
West Campus/Providence
   Services
500 15th Ave. S.
Great Falls, MT 59405

Saint Patrick Hospital and
   Health Sciences Center
500 W. Broadway
Missoula, MT 59801-4587
www.saintpatrick.org

Nebraska

Mary Lanning Memorial
   Hospital
715 N. St. Joseph Ave.
Hastings, NE 68901
www.mlmh.org

Southeast Community College
8800 O St.
Lincoln, NE 68520
www.southeast.edu

Alegent Health
7500 Mercy Rd.
Omaha, NE 68124
www.alegent.com

Clarkson College
101 S. 42nd St.
Omaha, NE 68131-2739
www.clarksoncollege.edu

University of Nebraska
   Medical Center
981045 Nebraska Medical
   Center
Omaha, NE 68198-1045
www.unmc.edu

Regional West Medical Center
4021 N. Ave. B
Scottsbluff, NE 69361
www.rwmc.net

Nevada

University of
   Nevada–Las Vegas
4505 Maryland Pkwy.
Las Vegas, NV 89154-3017
www.unlv.edu

Truckee Meadows
   Community College
7000 Dandini Blvd.
Reno, NV 89512-3999
www.tmcc.edu/x-ray

New Hampshire

New Hampshire Technical
   Institute
31 College Dr.
Concord, NH 03301-7412
www.nhti.edu

Lebanon College
15 Hanover St.
Lebanon, NH 03766
www.lebanoncollege.edu

New Jersey

Hudson Area School of
   Radiology Technology, Inc.
69-71 New Hook Rd.
Bayonne, NJ 07002

Cooper University
   Hospital/University
   Medical Center
1 Cooper Plaza
Camden, NJ 08103
www.cooperhealth.edu

Middlesex County College
2600 Woodbridge Ave.
P.O. Box 3050
Edison, NJ 08818-3050
www.middlesexcc.edu

Englewood Hospital and
Medical Center
350 Engle St.
Englewood, NJ 07631
www.englewoodhospital.com

Brookdale Community
College
765 Newman Springs Rd.
Lincroft, NJ 07738
www.brookdalecc.edu/fac/
radtech

St. Barnabas Medical Center
94 Old Short Hills Rd.
Livingston, NJ 07039
www.sbhcs.com

Essex County College
303 University Ave.
Newark, NJ 07102
www.essex.edu

Bergen Community College
400 Paramus Rd.
Paramus, NJ 07652-1595
www.bergen.cc.nj.us

Passaic County Community
College
1 College Blvd.
Paterson, NJ 07505-1179
www.pccc.cc.nj.us

Burlington County College
County Route 530
Pemberton, NJ 08068
www.bcc.edu

Muhlenberg Regional Medical
Center, Inc.
Park Ave. & Randolph Rd.
Plainfield, NJ 07061
www.muhlenbergschools.org

County College of Morris
214 Center Grove Rd.
Randolph, NJ 07869
www.ccm.edu

Valley Hospital
223 N. Van Dien Ave.
Ridgewood, NJ 07450-2736
www.valleyhealth.com

Shore Memorial Hospital
1 E. New York Ave.
Somers Point, NJ 08244-2387
www.shorememorial.org

Mercer County Community
    College
1200 Old Trenton Rd.
P.O. Box B
Trenton, NJ 08690
www.mccc.edu

St. Francis Medical Center
601 Hamilton Ave.
Trenton, NJ 08629-1986
www.stfrancismedical.com

Cumberland County College
P.O. Box 1500
Vineland, NJ 08362-1500
www.cccnj.edu

Pascack Valley Hospital
Old Hook Rd.
Westwood, NJ 07675-3181
www.pvhospital.org

New Mexico

Pima Medical Institute
2201 San Pedro NE, Bldg. 3,
    Ste. 100
Albuquerque, NM 87110
www.pimamedical.com

Clovis Community College
417 Schepps Blvd.
Clovis, NM 88101
www.clovis.edu

Northern New Mexico
    Community College
921 Paseo de Onate
Espanola, NM 87532
www.nnmcc.edu

Doña Ana Branch
    Community College
MSC 3DA
P.O. Box 30001
Las Cruces, NM 88003-8001
http://dabcc.nmsu.edu

New York

Broome Community College
Decker 217
Binghamton, NY 13902
www.sunybroome.edu

Bronx Community College of
    CUNY
University Ave. & West 181
    St., CPH 222
Bronx, NY 10453
www.bcc.cuny.edu

Hostos Community College
    of CUNY
475 Grand Concourse
Bronx, NY 10451
www.hostos.cuny.edu

Long Island College Hospital
339 Hicks St.
Brooklyn, NY 11201

New York City College of
Technology
300 Jay St.
Brooklyn, NY 11201-2983
www.citytech.cuny.edu

New York Methodist Hospital
506 6th St.
Brooklyn, NY 11215
www.nym.org

C. W. Post Campus
Long Island University
720 Northern Blvd.
Brookville, NY 11548-1300
www.liu.edu

Erie Community College,
City Campus
121 Ellicott St.
Buffalo, NY 14203
www.ecc.edu

Trocaire Junior College
360 Choate Ave.
Buffalo, NY 14220

Arnot-Ogden Medical Center
600 Roe Ave.
Elmira, NY 14905-1676

St. Vincent's Catholic Medical
Center of New York
175-05 H. Harding Expy.
Fresh Meadows, NY 11365

Nassau Community College
1 Education Dr.
Garden City, NY 11530
www.ncc.edu

Glens Falls Hospital
100 Park St.
Glens Falls, NY 12801
www.glensfallshospital.org

St. James Mercy Health
411 Canisteo St.
Hornell, NY 14843
www.stjamesmercy.org

Women's Christian
Association Hospital
207 Foote Ave.
Jamestown, NY 14701-0840
www.wcahospital.org

Orange County Community
College
115 South St.
Middletown, NY 10940
www.sunyorange.edu

Winthrop-University Hospital
259 First St.
Mineola, NY 11501
www.winthrop-radiology.com

Bellevue Hospital Center
1st Ave. & 27th St.
New York, NY 10016

Harlem Hospital Center
506 Lenox Ave.
Kountz Pavilion, 415
New York, NY 10037
www.harlemxray.com

Memorial Sloan-Kettering
    Cancer Center
1275 York Ave., Box 22
New York, NY 10021
www.mskcc.org

Northport VA Medical Center
79 Middleville Rd. (632/153)
Northport, NY 11768
www1.va.gov/visns/visn03/
    nrptinfo.asp

Robert J. Hochstim
School of Radiography
South Nassau Communities
    Hospital
1 Healthy Way
Oceanside, NY 11572

Champlain Valley Physicians
    Hospital
Medical Center
75 Beekman St.
Plattsburgh, NY 12901
www.cvph.org

Central Suffolk Hospital
1300 Roanoke Ave.
Riverhead, NY 11901
www.centralsuffolkhospital
    .org

Monroe Community College
1000 E. Henrietta Rd.
Rochester, NY 14623-5780
www.monroecc.edu

Mercy Medical Center
1000 N. Village Ave.
Rockville Centre, NY 11570
    516- 705- 2525
Niagara County Community
    College
3111 Saunders Settlement Rd.
Sanborn, NY 14132
www.niagaracc.suny.edu

North Country Community
    College
23 Santanoni Ave.
P.O. Box 89
Saranac Lake, NY 12983
www.nccc.edu

SUNY Upstate Medical
University
750 E. Adams St.
Syracuse, NY 13210
www.upstate.edu/chp/xray

St. Elizabeth Medical Center
2209 Genesee St.
Utica, NY 13501
www.stemc.org

St Luke's/Faxton–St. Luke's
Healthcare
Champlin Rd.
P.O. Box 479
Utica, NY 13503-0479

SUNY/Westchester
Community College
75 Grasslands Rd.
Valhalla, NY 10595
www.sunywcc.edu

St. Joseph's Medical Center
127 South Broadway
Yonkers, NY 10701

North Carolina

Asheville-Buncombe Technical
Community College
340 Victoria Rd.
Asheville, NC 28801
www.abtech.edu

University of North Carolina
at Chapel Hill
CB #7130 E Wing, Medical
School
Chapel Hill, NC 27599-7130
www.med.unc.edu/ahs/radisci

University of North Carolina
Hospitals
101 Manning Dr.
Chapel Hill, NC 27514-7512
www.unchealthcare.org

Carolinas College of Health
Science
P.O. Box 32861
Charlotte, NC 28232-2861
www.carolinascollege.edu

Presbyterian
Hospital/Presbyterian
Healthcare System
200 Hawthorne Ln.
P.O. Box 33549
Charlotte, NC 28233-3549
www.presbyterian.org

Fayetteville Technical
Community College
2201 Hull Rd.
P.O. Box 35236
Fayetteville, NC 28303-0236
www.faytechcc.edu

Moses H. Cone Memorial
Hospital
Moses Cone Health System
1200 N. Elm St.
Greensboro, NC 27401-1020
www.mosescone.com

Pitt Community College
P.O. Drawer 7007, Hwy. 11 S.
Greenville, NC 27835-7007
www.pittcc.edu

Vance-Granville Community
College
P.O. Box 917
Henderson, NC 27536
www.vgcc.cc.nc.us

Caldwell Community College
and Technical Institute
2855 Hickory Blvd.
Hudson, NC 28638
www.caldwell.cc.nc.us

Carteret Community College
3505 Arendell St.
Morehead City, NC 28557
www.carteret.edu

Wilkes Regional Medical
Center
P.O. Box 609
North Wilkesboro, NC 28659
www.wilkesregional.com

Sandhills Community College
2200 Airport Rd.
Pinehurst, NC 28374
www.sandhills.cc.nc.us

Wake Technical Community
College
9101 Fayetteville Rd.
Raleigh, NC 27603-5696
www.waketech.edu

Edgecombe Community
College
225 Tarboro St.
Rocky Mount, NC 27801
www.edgecombe.edu

Rowan-Cabarrus Community
College
P.O. Box 1595
Salisbury, NC 28145-1595
www.rowancabarrus.edu

Cleveland Community
College
137 S. Post Rd.
Shelby, NC 28150
www.cleveland.cc.nc.us

Johnston Community College
P.O. Box 2350
Smithfield, NC 27577-2350
www.johnstoncc.edu

Southwestern Community
College
447 College Dr.
Sylva, NC 28779
www.southwest.cc.nc.us

Cape Fear Community
College
411 N. Front St.
Wilmington, NC 28401
www.cfcc.edu

Forsyth Technical
Community College
2100 Silas Creek Pkwy.
Winston-Salem, NC 27103
www.forsythtech.edu

North Dakota

Medcenter One Health
Systems
300 N. 7th St.
Bismarck, ND 58506-5525
www.medcenterone.com

Trinity Hospital
407 3rd St. SE, Box 5020
Minot, ND 58701

MeritCare Medical Center
720 4th St. N., Rt. #714
North Fargo, ND 58122
www.meritcare.com

Ohio

Children's Hospital Medical
Center of Akron
1 Perkins Sq.
Akron, OH 44308
www.akronchildrens.org

Aultman Hospital
2600 6th St. SW
Canton, OH 44710
www.aultman.com

Mercy Medical Center
1320 Mercy Dr. NW
Canton, OH 44708
www.thequalityhospital.com

University of Cincinnati
Raymond Walters College
9555 Plainfield Rd.
Cincinnati, OH 45236-1096
www.rwc.uc.edu

Xavier University
3800 Victory Pkwy.
Cincinnati, OH 45207-4331
www.xu.edu

Cleveland Clinic Foundation
9500 Euclid Ave. (T28)
Cleveland, OH 44195
www.clevelandclinic.org/
education

Arthur G. James Cancer
Hospital
Richard J. Solove Research
Institute
300 W. 10th Ave.
Columbus, OH 43210
www.radiationtherapy.osu.edu

Columbus State Community
College
550 E. Spring St.
Columbus, OH 43215
www.cscc.edu/ah

Sinclair Community College
444 W. Third St.
Dayton, OH 45402-1460
www.sinclair.edu/depart
ments/rat

Lorain County Community
College
1005 N. Abbe Rd.
Elyria, OH 44035
www.lorainccc.edu

Euclid Hospital
Cleveland Clinic Health
System
18901 Lakeshore Blvd.
Euclid, OH 44119
www.euclidhospital.org

Kettering College of Medical
Arts
3737 Southern Blvd.
Kettering, OH 45429
www.kcma.edu

Lakeland Community College
7700 Clocktower Dr.
Kirtland, OH 44094-5198
www.lakelandcc.edu

James A. Rhodes State College
4240 Campus Dr.
Lima, OH 45804-3597
www.rhodesstate.edu

North Central Technical
College
2441 Kenwood Cir.
P.O. Box 698
Mansfield, OH 44901-0698
www.ncstatecollege.edu

Marietta Memorial Hospital
401 Matthew St.
Marietta, OH 45750
www.mmhospital.org

Marion Technical College
1467 Mt. Vernon Ave.
Marion, OH 43302-5694
www.mtc.edu

Central Ohio Technical
College
1179 University Dr.
Newark, OH 43055-1767
www.cotc.edu

Cuyahoga Community
College (Western Campus)
11000 Pleasant Valley Rd.
Parma, OH 44130-5199
www.tri-c.edu/home/default
.htm

Shawnee State University
940 Second St.
Portsmouth, OH 45662-4344
www.shawnee.edu

Kent State University (Salem
Campus)
2491 S.R. 45 S.
Salem, OH 44460-9412
www.salem.kent.edu

Firelands Regional Medical
Center
School of Radiologic
Technology
1912 Hayes Ave.
Sandusky, OH 44870
www.firelands.com

Jefferson Community College
4000 Sunset Blvd.
Steubenville, OH 43952-3598
http://ns3.jeffersoncc.org/jcc/
default.htm

Mercy College of Northwest
Ohio
2221 Madison Ave.
Toledo, OH 43624-1132
www.mercycollege.edu

Owens Community College
P.O. Box 10,000
Toledo, OH 43699-1947
www.owens.edu

Zane State College
1555 Newark Rd.
Zanesville, OH 43701
www.zanestate.edu

Oklahoma

Western Oklahoma State
College
2801 N. Main
Altus, OK 73521-1397
www.wosc.edu

Autry Technology Center
1201 W. Willow
Enid, OK 73703
www.autrytech.com

Great Plains Technology
    Center
4500 W. Lee Blvd.
Lawton, OK 73505
www.gptech.org

Rose State College
6420 SE 15th St.
Midwest City, OK 73110
www.rose.edu

Bacone College
2299 Old Bacone Rd.
Muskogee, OK 74403-1597
www.bacone.edu

Indian Capital Technology
    Center
2403 N. 41st St. E.
Muskogee, OK 74403-1799
www.icavts.tec.ok.us

Metro Technology Centers
School District #22
1720 Springlake Dr.
Oklahoma City, OK 73111
www.metrotech.org

University of Oklahoma
    Health Sciences Center
P.O. Box 26901, CHB 451
Oklahoma City, OK 73190
www.ah.ouhsc.edu/radtech

Carl Albert State College
1507 S. McKenna
Poteau, OK 74953
www.carlalbert.edu

Southwestern Oklahoma State
    University at Sayre
409 E. Mississippi
Sayre, OK 73662-1236
www.swosu.edu

Meridian Technology Center
1312 S. Sangre Rd.
Stillwater, OK 74074-1899
www.meridian-technology
    .com

Tulsa Community College
Metro Campus, Allied Health
    Division
909 S. Boston Ave.
Tulsa, OK 74119
www.tulsacc.edu

Tulsa Technology Center
School District No. 18
801 E. 91st St.
Tulsa, OK 74132-4008
www.tulsatech.com

Oregon

Oregon Health and Science
University
3181 SW Sam Jackson Park
Rd., GH119
Portland, OR 97239-3098
www.ohsu.edu

Portland Community College
P.O. Box 19000 SY HT 306
Portland, OR 97280-0990
www.pcc.edu

Pennsylvania

Northampton Community
College
3835 Green Pond Rd.
Bethlehem, PA 18020
www.northhampton.edu

Bradford Regional Medical
Center
116 Interstate Pkwy.
Bradford, PA 16701
www.brmc.com

Bryn Mawr Hospital/Main
Line Health
130 S. Bryn Mawr Ave.
Bryn Mawr, PA 19010

Holy Spirit Hospital
503 N. 21st St.
Camp Hill, PA 17011-2288
www.hsh.org/home.htm

Clearfield Hospital
809 Turnpike Ave.
P.O. Box 992
Clearfield, PA 16830
www.clearfieldhosp.org

College Misericordia
301 Lake St.
Dallas, PA 18612
www.misericordia.edu

Geisinger Medical Center
100 N. Academy Ave.
Danville, PA 17822-2007
www.geisinger.org

Gannon University
109 University Sq.
Erie, PA 16541-0001
www.gannon.edu

Gwynedd-Mercy College
P.O. Box 901
Gwynedd Valle, PA 19437-
0901
www.gmc.edu

Pinnacle Health School of
Radiology
P.O. Box 8700
Harrisburg, PA 17105-8700

St. Joseph Medical Center
687 N. Church St.
Hazleton, PA 18201-3198
www.ghha.org

Conemaugh Memorial
Medical Center
1086 Franklin St.
Johnstown, PA 15905-4398
www.conemaugh.org

Armstrong County Memorial
Hospital
1 Nolte Dr.
Kittanning, PA 16201
www.acmh.org

Lancaster General College of
Nursing and Health
Sciences
410 N. Lime St.
Lancaster, PA 17602
www.allalliedhealthschools
.com/schools/id1486

Mansfield University
Elliott Hall
Mansfield, PA 16933
www.mnsfld.edu

Ohio Valley General Hospital
La Roche College
25 Heckel Rd.
McKees Rocks, PA 15136
www.ohiovalleyhospital.org

Community College of
Allegheny County
Boyce Campus
595 Beatty Rd.
Monroeville, PA 15146-1395
www.ccac.edu

Jameson Hospital, North
Campus
1211 Wilmington Ave.
New Castle, PA 16105
www.jamesonhealthsystem
.com

Bucks County Community
College
275 Swamp Rd.
Tyler Hall 302A
Newtown, PA 18940
www.bucks.edu/healthcare/
radiography

Albert Einstein Medical
Center
5501 Old York Rd.
Philadelphia, PA 19141
www.einsteinxray.org

Community College of
Philadelphia
1700 Spring Garden St.
Philadelphia, PA 19130-3991
www.ccp.edu

Drexel University
245 N. 15th St.
Mail Stop 507
Philadelphia, PA 19102-1192
www.drexel.edu

Holy Family University
Grant & Frankford Aves.
Philadelphia, PA 19114
www.holyfamily.edu

St. Christopher's Hospital for
Children
240 E. Erie Ave.
Philadelphia, PA 19134-1095
www.stchristophershospital
.com

Thomas Jefferson University
130 S. 9th St., Ste. 1010
Philadelphia, PA 19107-5233
www.tju.edu/chp

University of Pennsylvania
M.C./Hospital of the
University of Pennsylvania
3400 Spruce St.
Basement Donner Bldg.
Philadelphia, PA 19104
www.uphs.upenn.edu/
radiology

Community College of
Allegheny County
Allegheny Campus
808 Ridge Ave.
Pittsburgh, PA 15212-6097
www.ccac.edu

UPMC Presbyterian
Shadyside
UPMC Health System
3434 Forbes Ave.
Pittsburgh, PA 15213-2582
www.upmc.edu

Western School of Health and
Business Careers
421 7th Ave.
Pittsburgh, PA 15219
www.western-school.com

Montgomery County
Community College
101 College Dr.
Pottstown, PA 19464
www.mc3.edu/aa/career/
programs/rt.htm

The Reading Hospital and
Medical Center
P.O. Box 16052
Reading, PA 19612-6052
www.readinghospital.org

St. Joseph Medical Center
12th and Walnut St.
P.O. Box 316
Reading, PA 19603

Pennsylvania State University
200 University Dr.
Schuylkill Haven, PA 17972
www.sl.psu.edu

Johnson College
3427 N. Main Ave.
Scranton, PA 18508-1495
www.johnson.edu

UPMC Northwest
100 Fairfield Dr.
Seneca, PA 16346
http://northwest.upmc.com

Sewickley Valley Hospital
720 Blackburn Rd.
Sewickley, PA 15143-1498

Sharon Regional Health
System
740 E. State St.
Sharon, PA 16146-3395
www.sharonregional.com

Crozer-Chester Medical
Center
1 Medical Center Blvd.
Upland, PA 19013
www.crozer.org

Pennsylvania State University
3550 7th Street Rd.
Upper Burrell, PA 15068-
1798
www.nk.psu.edu

Washington Hospital
155 Wilson Ave.
Washington, PA 15301
www.washingtonhospital.org

Wilkes-Barre General
Hospital
Wyoming Valley Healthcare
System, Inc.
575 N. River St.
Wilkes-Barre, PA 18764
http://www.wvhcs.org

Pennsylvania College of
Technology
1 College Ave.
Williamsport, PA 17701-5799
www.pct.edu/schools/hs/
radiography

Abington Memorial Hospital
2500 Maryland Rd.
Willow Grove, PA 19090
www.amh.org

Puerto Rico

School of Radiography
Universidad Central Del
Caribe
Call Box 60-327
Bayamon, PR 00960
www.uccaribe.edu

School of Radiography
University of Puerto Rico
Med. Sci. Campus
P.O. Box 365067
San Juan, PR 00936-5067

Rhode Island

Community College of Rhode
Island
1762 Louisquisset Pike
Lincoln, RI 02865-4585
www.ccri.edu

Rhode Island Hospital
3 Davol Sq.
Bldg. A, 4th Fl.
Providence, RI 02903

South Carolina

Aiken Technical College
P.O. Drawer 696
Aiken, SC 29802-0696
www.aik.tec.sc.us

Anderson Area Medical
Center
800 N. Fant St.
Anderson, SC 29621

Technical College of the
Lowcountry
P.O. Box 1288
Beaufort, SC 29901
www.tcl.edu

Trident Technical College
7000 Rivers Ave.
P.O. Box 118067
Charleston, SC 29423-8067
www.tridenttech.edu

Midlands Technical College
P.O. Box 2408
Columbia, SC 29202
www.mid.tec.sc.us

Horry-Georgetown Technical
College
2050 Hwy. 501 E.
P.O. Box 261966
Conway, SC 29528-6066
www.hor.tec.sc.us

Florence-Darlington Technical
College
P.O. Drawer 100548
Florence, SC 29501-0548
www.fdtc.edu

Greenville Technical College
506 S. Pleasantburg Dr.
Greenville, SC 29607
www.greenvilletech.com

Piedmont Technical College
Drawer 1467
Greenwood, SC 29648
www.ptc.edu

Orangeburg-Calhoun
Technical College
3250 St. Matthews Rd.
Orangeburg, SC 29118-8299
www.octech.edu

York Technical College
452 S. Anderson Rd.
Rock Hill, SC 29730
www.yorktech.com

Spartanburg Technical College
P.O. Box 4386
Spartanburg, SC 29303-4386
www.stcsc.edu/hhs/rad

South Dakota

Presentation College
1500 N. Main St.
Aberdeen, SD 57401
www.presentation.edu

Mitchell Technical Institute
821 N. Capital
Mitchell, SD 57301
www.mitchelltech.com

Rapid City Regional Hospital
353 Fairmont Blvd.
Rapid City, SD 57709-6000
www.rcrh.org

Avera McKennan Hospital
P.O. Box 5045
Sioux Falls, SD 57117-5045
www.mckennan.org

Sioux Valley Hospital
1305 W. 18th St.
P.O. Box 5039
Sioux Falls, SD 57105
www.siouxvalley.org

Avera Sacred Heart Hospital
501 Summit
Yankton, SD 57078-9967
www.averasacredheart.com

Tennessee

Chattanooga State Technical
Community College
4501 Amnicola Hwy.
Chattanooga, TN 37406
www.chattanoogastate.edu

Columbia State Community
College
1665 Hampshire Pike
P.O. Box 1315
Columbia, TN 38402-1315
www.columbiastate.edu

MedVance
Institute–Cookeville
KIMC Investments, Inc.
1025 Hwy. 111
Cookeville, TN 38501
www.medvance.org

East Tennessee State
University
Nave Center, 1000 W. E St.
Elizabethton, TN 37643
www.etsu.edu

Volunteer State Community
College
1480 Nashville Pike
Gallatin, TN 37066-3188
www.volstate.edu

Jackson State Community
College
2046 N. Parkway St.
Jackson, TN 38301-3797
www.jscc.edu

South College
720 N. Fifth Ave.
Knoxville, TN 37917
www.southcollege.edu

University of Tennessee
Medical Center at Knoxville
1924 Alcoa Hwy.
Knoxville, TN 37920-6999
www.utmedicalcenter.org

Baptist Memorial College of
Health Sciences
1003 Monroe Ave., 3rd Fl.
Memphis, TN 38104
www.bchs.edu

Methodist University
Methodist Healthcare
1265 Union Ave.
Memphis, TN 38104
www.methodisthealth.org

Southwest Tennessee
  Community College
Allied Health Building, Union
  Campus
P.O. Box 780
Memphis, TN 38101-0780
www.southwest.tn.edu

Nashville General Hospital
1818 Albion St.
Nashville, TN 37208
www.nashville.gov/general
  _hospital

Vanderbilt Center for
  Radiation Oncology
1301 22nd Ave. South,
  B-902 TVC
Nashville, TN 37232-5671
www.mc.vanderbilt.edu

Roane State Community
  College
701 Briarcliff Ave.
Oak Ridge, TN 37830
www.roanestate.edu/rdt

Texas

Hendrick Medical Center
1900 Pine St.
Abilene, TX 79601-2316
www.ehendrick.org/
  radiography

Amarillo College
P.O. Box 447
Amarillo, TX 79178
www.actx.edu

Austin Community College
Eastview Campus
3401 Webberville Rd.
Austin, TX 78702
www.austincc.edu/hltsci/rad

Memorial Hermann Baptist
  Hospital–Beaumont
P.O. Drawer 1591
Beaumont, TX 77704
www.memorialhermann.org

Lamar Institute of Technology
P.O. Box 10061
Beaumont, TX 77710
www.lit.edu

Scenic Mountain Medical
  Center
1601 W. 11th Pl.
Big Spring, TX 79720-9990
www.smmccares.com

University of Texas at
  Brownsville
Texas Southmost College
80 Ft. Brown
Brownsville, TX 78520-4993
www.utb.edu

Blinn College
P.O. Box 6030
Bryan, TX 77805-6030
www.blinn.edu

Montgomery College
3200 College Park Dr.
Conroe, TX 77384
wwwmc.nhmccd.edu/
   templates/content.aspx
   ?pid=1929

Del Mar College
101 Baldwin
Corpus Christi, TX 78404
www.delmar.edu

Baylor University Medical
   Center
3616 Worth Ave.
Dallas, TX 75246
www.baylorhealth.edu/rahs

El Centro College
Main & Lamar Sts.
Dallas, TX 75202-3604
www.elcentrocollege.edu

El Paso Community College
P.O. Box 20500
El Paso, TX 79998
www.epcc.edu

U.S. Army Medical Dept.
   Center & School
Department of Clinical
   Support Services
3151 Scott Rd.,
   1334 MCCS-HCR
Fort Sam Houston, TX 78234
http://radiology.amedd.army
   .mil

JPS Institute of Health Career
   Development
2400 Circle Dr., Ste. 100
Fort Worth, TX 76119
www.jpshealthnet.org

Galveston College
4015 Ave. Q
Galveston, TX 77550-2782
www.gc.edu

Harris County Hospital
   District
Ben Taub General Hospital
1504 Taub Loop
Houston, TX 77030
www.hchdonline.com

Houston Community College
   System
1900 Pressler St.
   (1637-H512)
Houston, TX 77030
www.hccs.cc.tx.us

MedVance Institute–Houston
KIMC Investments, Inc.
6220 Westpark, Ste. 180
Houston, TX 77057
www.medvance.org

Memorial City Hospital
Memorial Hermann
    Healthcare Hospital
920 Frostwood
Houston, TX 77024
www.memorialhermann.org

University of Texas
M. D. Anderson Cancer
    Center
1515 Holcombe Blvd., Unit
    190
Houston, TX 77030
www.mdanderson.org/health
    sciences

Tarrant County College
    (Northeast Campus)
828 Harwood Rd.
Hurst, TX 76054-3299
www.tccd.edu

Laredo Community College
West End Washington St.
Laredo, TX 78040-4395
www.laredo.edu

Covenent Medical Center
3706 20th St., Ste. A
Lubbock, TX 79410
www.covenantsor.com

South Plains College, Reese
    Center
819 Gilbert Dr.
Lubbock, TX 79416-2120
www.southplainscollege.edu

Angelina College
3500 S. First St.
P.O. Box 1768
Lufkin, TX 75901-1768
www.angelina.cc.tx.us

Midland College
3600 N. Garfield
Midland, TX 79705-6399
www.midland.edu

Odessa College
201 W. University Blvd.
Odessa, TX 79764
www.odessa.edu

San Jacinto College Central
8060 Spencer Hwy.
P.O. Box 2007
Pasadena, TX 77501-2007
www.sjcd.edu

Baptist Medical Center
Vanguard Health Systems
730 N. Main, Ste. 212,
   M&S Tower
San Antonio, TX 78205-1115
www.vanguardhealth.com/
   hosp_txbaptmed.html

St. Philip's College
1801 Martin Luther King Dr.
San Antonio, TX 78203-2098
www.accd.edu/spc/spcmain/
   spc.htm

Texas State University–San
   Marcos
601 University Dr. HSC
   350B
San Marcos, TX 78666
www.health.txstate.edu/rtt

School of Health Care
   Sciences/USAF
917 Missile Rd.
382 TRS/XYAF
Diagnostic Imaging Course
Sheppard AFB, TX 76311

Tyler Junior College
P.O. Box 9020
Tyler, TX 75711
www.tjc.edu/radtech/radtech
   .htm

Citizens Medical Center
2701 Hospital Dr.
Victoria, TX 77901
www.citizensmedicalcenter.org

McLennan Community
   College
1400 College Dr.
Waco, TX 76708
www.mclennan.edu/depart
   ments/hsp/rtp

Wharton County Junior
   College
911 Boling Hwy.
Wharton, TX 77488
www.wcjc.cc.tx.us

Midwestern State University
3410 Taft Blvd.
Wichita Falls, TX 76308
http://hs2.mwsu.edu/radsci

Utah

Salt Lake Community College
South City Campus
1575 S. State St.
Salt Lake City, UT 84115
www.slcc.edu/pages/1035.asp

Vermont

Champlain College
163 S. Willard St.
P.O. Box 670
Burlington, VT 05402-0670
www.champlain.edu

New England School of
    Radiologic Technology
160 Allen St.
Rutland, VT 05701

Virginia

University of Virginia Medical
    Center
University of Virginia Health
    System
Radiology Box 800377
Charlottesville, VA 22908-
    0377
www.med.virginia.edu

Danville Regional Medical
    Center
Danville Regional Health
    System
142 S. Main St.
Danville, VA 24541
www.danvilleregional.org

Mary Washington Hospital
1001 Sam Perry Blvd.
Fredericksburg, VA 22401
www.medicorp.org/mwh

Rockingham Memorial
    Hospital
235 Cantrell Ave.
Harrisonburg, VA 22801-
    3293

Central Virginia Community
    College
3506 Wards Rd.
Lynchburg, VA 24502-2498
www.cv.vccs.edu

Riverside Hospital
Riverside Health System
310 Main St.
Newport News, VA 23601-
    3814
www.riverside-online.com/
    rshc

Southside Regional Medical
    Center
Community Health Systems,
    Inc.
801 S. Adams St.
Petersburg, VA 23803
www.srmconline.com

Naval School of Health
    Sciences
1001 Holcomb Rd.
Portsmouth, VA 23708-5200

Southwest Virginia
    Community College
Box SVCC
Richlands, VA 24641
www.sw.edu

Bon Secours St. Mary's
    Hospital
8550 Magellan Pkwy.,
    Ste. 1100
Richmond, VA 23227
www.bonsecours.com/smh/
    default.asp

Virginia Commonwealth
    University
P.O. Box 843057
Richmond, VA 23284-3057
www.vcu.edu

Virginia Western Community
    College
3095 Colonial Ave.
P.O. Box 14007
Roanoke, VA 24038
www.vw.vccs.edu

Tidewater Community
    College
1700 College Crescent
Virginia Beach, VA 23453
www.tcc.edu

Winchester Medical Center,
    Inc.
1840 Amherst St.
P.O. Box 3340
Winchester, VA 22601

Washington

Bellevue Community College
3000 Landerholm Circle SE,
    B-243
Bellevue, WA 98007-6484
www.bcc.ctc.edu/radonpima

Medical Institute
1627 Eastlake Ave. E.
Seattle, WA 98102

Apollo College–Spokane
U.S. Education Corporation
10102 E. Knox Rd., Ste. 200
Spokane, WA 99206
www.apollocollege.edu

Sacred Heart Medical Center
101 W. 8th Ave.
Spokane, WA 99204
www.shmc.org

Tacoma Community College
6501 S. 19th St., Bldg. 19
Tacoma, WA 98466
www.tacoma.ctc.edu

Yakima Valley Community
    College
16th Ave. & Nob Hill Blvd.
P.O. Box 22520
Yakima, WA 98907-2520
www.yvcc.edu

West Virginia

Mountain State University
Box 9003
Beckley, WV 25802-9003
www.mountainstate.edu

Bluefield State College
219 Rock St.
Bluefield, WV 24701
www.bluefieldstate.edu

University of Charleston
2300 MacCorkle Ave. SE
Charleston, WV 25304
www.ucwv.edu/dhs/radsci

United Hospital Center
#3 Hospital Plaza
Rt. 19 South
Clarksburg, WV 26302-1680
www.uhcwv.org

St. Mary's Medical Center
2900 First Ave.
Huntington, WV 25702
www.stmarys.org

West Virginia University
    Hospitals, Inc.
Medical Center Dr.
P.O. Box 8150
Morgantown, WV 26506-
    8150
www.wvuhradtech.com

Southern West Virginia
    Community and Technical
    College
P.O. Box 2900
Mt. Gay, WV 25637
www.southern.wvnet.edu

Ohio Valley Medical Center,
    Inc.
2000 Eoff St.
Wheeling, WV 26003
www.ohiovalleymedicalcenter
    .com

Wheeling Hospital
1 Medical Park
Wheeling, WV 26003-0668
www.wheelinghospital.com

Wisconsin

Lakeshore Technical College
1290 North Ave.
Cleveland, WI 53015-1414
www.gotoltc.com

Chippewa Valley Technical
College
620 W. Clairemont Ave.
Eau Claire, WI 54701-6162
www.cvtc.edu

Bellin Health Hospital
Bellin Health Systems, Inc.
P.O. Box 23400
Green Bay, WI 54305-3400
www.bellin.org/careers

Blackhawk Technical College
P.O. Box 5009
Janesville, WI 53547
www.blackhawk.edu

University of Wisconsin
1725 State St. (4094 HSC)
LaCrosse, WI 54601
www.uwlax.edu/rt

Western Wisconsin Technical
College
P.O. Box 908
LaCrosse, WI 54602-0908
www.wwtc.edu/rad

Madison Area Technical
College
3550 Anderson St.
Madison, WI 53704-2599
www.matcmadison.edu/
radiography

University of Wisconsin
Hospital & Clinics
600 Highland Ave., E3/311
Radiology
Madison, WI 53792-3252
www.uwhealth.org/healthprof

St. Joseph's Hospital
611 St. Joseph Ave.
Marshfield, WI 54449
www.stjosephs-marshfield.org

Columbia/St. Mary's Hospitals
2025 E. Newport Ave.
Milwaukee, WI 53211
www.columbia-stmarys.org

Froedtert Memorial Lutheran
    Hospital
9200 W. Wisconsin Ave.
Milwaukee, WI 53226
www.froedtert.com

Milwaukee Area Technical
    College
700 W. State St.
Milwaukee, WI 53233-1443
www.milwaukee.tec.wi.us

St. Luke's Medical Center,
    Airport
180 W. Grange Ave.
Milwaukee, WI 53207

St. Michael Hospital
2400 W. Villard Ave.
Milwaukee, WI 53209

Theda Clark Medical Center
130 Second St.
P.O. Box 2021
Neenah, WI 54956-2021

Mercy Medical Center
Affinity Health System
500 S. Oakwood Rd.
Oshkosh, WI 54904
www.affinityhealth.org/object/
    mmchospital.html

St. Mary's Campus
All Saints Healthcare
3801 Spring St.
Racine, WI 53405

Northcentral Technical
    College
1000 W. Campus Dr.
Wausau, WI 54401-1899
www.ntc.edu

Wyoming

Casper College
125 College Dr.
Casper, WY 82601
www.caspercollege.edu

Laramie County Community
    College
1400 E. College Dr.
Cheyenne, WY 82007
www.lccc.wy.edu/radiography

Appendix C

Accredited Diagnostic Medical Sonographer Programs

Alabama

Wallace State College
DMS Program
P.O. Box 2000
Hanceville, AL 35077
www.wallacestate.edu

Institute of Ultrasound
    Diagnostics
1230 Montlimar Dr., Ste. A
Mobile, AL 36527

Baptist Medical Center South
2169 Normandie Dr.
Montogomery, AL 36111
http://baptistfirst.org/
    facilities/south.htm

Arizona

Gateway Community College
108 N. 40th St.
Phoenix, AZ 85034
www.gatewaycc.edu

Pima Medical Institute
3350 E. Grant Rd.
Tucson, AZ 85716
www.pimamedical.com/
    locations/tucson.asp

Arkansas

University of Arkansas for
    Medical Sciences
4301 W. Markham St.
Little Rock, AR 72205
http://uams.edu

California

Orange Coast College
Diagnostic Medical
   Sonographers Program
2701 Fairview Rd.
Costa Mesa, CA 92628
www.orangecoastcollege.edu

Cypress College
920 Valley View St.
Cypress, CA 90630
http://cypresscollege.edu

Loma Linda University
School of Allied Health
   Professionals
Diagnostic Medical
   Sonographer Program
Loma Linda, CA 92350
http://llu.edu

Foothill College
12345 El Monte Rd.
Los Altos Hills, CA 94022
http://foothill.fhda.edu/index
   .php

Kaiser Permanente School of
   Allied Health Sciences
901 Nevis Ave.
Richmond, CA 94801
http://kpsahs.org

University of California San
   Diego Medical Center
200 W. Arbor Dr.
San Diego, CA 92103
http://health.ucsd.edu/default
   .htm

Colorado

University of Colorado
   Hospital
Anschutz Centers for
   Advanced Medicine
1635 N. Ursula St.
Denver, CO 80262
www.uch.edu

Connecticut

St. Francis Hospital and
   Medical Center
114 Woodland St.
Hartford, CT 06105
www.stfranciscare.org/
   homepage.cfm

Yale–New Haven Hospital
20 York St., Rm. SP 2122
New Haven, CT 90630
www.ynhh.org

Delaware

Delaware Technical and
    Community College
333 Shipley St.
Wilmington, DE 19801
www.dtcc.edu

District of Columbia

George Washington
    University
Diagnostic Medical
    Sonographer Program
900 23rd St. NE, #6180
Washington, DC 20037
www.gwumc.edu/healthsci/
    programs/sono/sono
    _programinfo.htm

Florida

Broward Community College
Diagnostic Medical
    Sonography Program
Health Sciences II, North
    Campus Bldg. 41
Coconut Creek, FL 33066
www.broward.edu

Keiser College–Daytona
    Beach
1800 Business Park Blvd.
Daytona Beach, FL 32114
www.keisercollege.cc.fl.us/
    daytona.htm

Keiser College–Ft. Lauderdale
1500 NW 49th St.
Ft. Lauderdale, FL 33309
www.keisercollege.edu

St. Vincent's Medical Center
1800 Barrs St.
Jacksonville, FL 32204
www.jaxhealth.com/aboutus/
    default.asp

Miami Dade College
Medical Center Campus
Miami, FL 33127
www.mdc.edu

Florida Hospital College of
    Health Sciences
800 Lake Estelle Dr.
Orlando, FL 32803
www.fhchs.edu

Valencia Community College
P.O. Box 3028
Orlando, FL 32802
www.valencia.cc.fl.us

Hillsborough Community
    College
Diagnostic Medical
    Sonographer Program
P.O. Box 30030
Tampa, FL 33630
www.hccfl.edu

Georgia

Grady Health System
Box 26095
Atlanta, GA 03
www.gradyhealthsystem.org/
    index1.asp

Sanford Brown Institute
1140 Hamond Dr.,
    Ste. A-115
Atlanta, GA 30328

Medical College of Georgia
Diagnostic Medical
    Sonographer Program
1120 15th St., AE 1012
Augusta, GA 30912
www.mcg.edu

Coose Valley Technical
    College
1 Maurice Culberson Dr.
Rome, GA 30161

Ogeechee Technical College
1 Joe Kennedy Blvd.
Statesboro, GA 30458
www.ogeechee.tec.ga.us

Iowa

Mercy College of Health
    Sciences
928 6th Ave.
Des Moines, IA 50309
www.mchs.edu

University of Iowa Healthcare
Diagnostic Medical
    Sonographer Program
Radiology Dept., C723
Iowa City, IA 52242
www.uihealthcare.com

Idaho

Boise State University
1910 University Dr.
Boise, ID 83725
www.boisestate.edu

Illinois

John A. Logan College
700 Logan College Rd.
Carterville, IL 62918
www.jal.cc.il.us

College of DuPage
425 Fawell Blvd.
Glen Ellyn, IL 60137
www.cod.edu

Triton College
2000 N. Fifth Ave.
River Grove, IL 60171
www.triton.cc.il.us

South Suburban College of
Cook County
15800 S. State St.
South Holland, IL 60473
www.ssc.cc.il.us

Kansas

University of Kansas Medical
Center
3901 Rainbow Blvd.
Kansas City, KS 66160
www.kumc.edu

Kentucky

St. Catherine College,
Bardstown Program
310 Xavier Dr.
Bardstown, KY 40004
www.sccky.edu

Bowling Green Technical
College
1845 Loop Dr.
Bowling Green, KY 42101
www.bowlinggreen.kctcs.edu

West Kentucky State
Vocational Technical
Diagnostic Medical
Sonographer Program
Blandville Rd.
P.O. Box 7308
Paducah, KY 42002
www.westkentucky.kctcs.edu

Louisiana

Louisiana State University at
Eunice
P.O. Box 1129
Eunice, LA 70535
www.lsue.edu

Delgado Community College
615 City Park Ave.
New Orleans, LA 70119
www.dcc.edu

Maryland

Johns Hopkins Hospital
Blalock B-179
Baltimore, MD 21287
www.hopkinsmedicine.org/
     organizations/jhhospital

University of Maryland
     Baltimore County
3108 Lord Baltimore Dr.
Baltimore, MD 21224
www.umbc.edu

Montgomery College
7977 Georgia Ave., #437
Silver Spring, MD 20910
www.montgomerycollege.edu

Massachusetts

Middlesex Community
     College
Diagnostic Medical
     Sonographer Program
Springs Rd.
Bedford, MA 01730
www.mxctc.commnet.edu

Bunker Hill Community
     College
250 New Rutherford Ave.
Boston, MA 02129
www.bhcc.mass.edu

Springfield Technical
     Community College
1 Armory Sq.
Springfield, MA 01105
www.stcc.edu

Michigan

Oakland Community College
Diagnostic Medical
     Sonographer Program
2480 Opdyke Rd.
Bloomfield Hills, MI 48304
www.oaklandcc.edu

Henry Ford Hospital
Diagnostic Medical
     Sonographer Program
2799 W. Grand Blvd.
Detroit, MI 48202
www.henryfordhealth.org/
     body.cfm?id=37471

Jackson Community College
Diagnostic Medical
     Sonographer Program
2111 Emmons Rd.
Jackson, MI 49201
www.jackson.cc.mi.us

Lansing Community College
P.O. Box 40010, Mail Code
2000
Lansing, MI 48901
www.lansing.cc.mi.us

Providence Hospital
16001 W. Nine Mile Rd.
Southfield, MI 48037
www.realmedicine.org/
providence

Delta College
1961 Delta Rd.
University Center, MI 48710
www.delta.edu

Minnesota

Argosy University/Twin Cities
1515 Central Pkwy.
Eagan, MN 55121
www.aspp.edu

The College of St. Catherine's
601 25th Ave. S.
Minneapolis, MN 55454
www.stkate.edu

Mayo Foundation
Diagnostic Medical
Sonographer Program
200 First St. SW
Rochester, MN 55905
www.mayo.edu

Missouri

St. Louis Community College
at Forest Park
Diagnostic Medical
Sonography Program
5600 Oakland Ave.
St. Louis, MO 63110
www.stlcc.cc.mo.us/fp

Cox Health Systems
3801 S. National Ave.
Springfield, MO 65807
www.coxhealth.com

Mississippi

Itawamba Community
College
2176 S. Eason Blvd.
Tupelo, MS 38804
www.icc.cc.ms.us

Nebraska

Nebraska Methodist College
of Nursing and Allied
Health
8501 W. Dodge Rd.
Omaha, NE 68114
www.methodistcollege.edu

University of Nebraska
Medical Center
600 S. 42nd St.
Omaha, NE 68198
www.unmc.edu

New Hampshire

New Hampshire Technical
Institute
11 Institute Dr.
Concord, NH 03317
www.nhti.edu

New Jersey

Sanford Brown Institute
675 US Hwy. #1
Plaza Gill Lane, 2nd Fl.
Iselin, NJ 08830

University of Medicine and
Dentistry of New Jersey
School of Health Related
Professions
Diagnostic Medical
Sonography Program
65 Bergen St.
Newark, NJ 07107
www.umdnj.edu

Bergen County Community
College
Diagnostic Medical
Sonography Program
400 Paramus Rd.
Paramus, NJ 07652-1595
www.bergen.cc.nj.us

Muhlenberg Regional Medical
Center
Harold B. & Dorothy A.
Snyder Schools
Park Ave. and Randolph Rd.
Plainfield, NJ 07061
www.muhlenberg.com

Gloucester County College
1400 Tanyard Rd.
Sewell, NJ 08080
www.gccnj.edu

New Mexico

Albuquerque Technical
   Vocational Institute
525 Buena Vista SE
Albuquerque, NM 87106
www.tvi.cc.nm.us

New York

SUNY Downstate Medical
   Center
450 Clarkson Ave.
Brooklyn, NY 11203
www.hscbklyn.edu

New York University
594 Broadway
New York, NY 10012
www.nyu.edu

Western Suffolk BOCES
Northport VA Medical Center
152 Laurel Hill Rd.
Northport, NY 11748

Rochester Institute of
   Technology
Diagnostic Medical
   Sonographer Program
85 Memorial Dr.
Rochester, NY 14623
www.rit.edu

Hudson Valley Community
   College
80 Vandenburgh Ave.
Troy, NY 12180
www.hvcc.edu

North Carolina

Asheville-Buncombe Technical
   Community College
340 Victoria Rd.
Asheville, NC 28801
www.abtech.edu

Pitt Community College
Diagnostic Medical
   Sonography Program
P.O. Drawer 7007
Greenville, NC 27835
www.pitt.cc.nc.us

Caldwell Community College
   and Technical Institute
Diagnostic Medical
   Sonographer Program
2855 Hickory Blvd.
Hudson, NC 28638
www.caldwell.cc.nc.us

South Piedmont Community
   College
4209 Old Charlotte Hwy.
Monroe, NC 28110
www.spcc.edu

Johnson Community College
P.O. Box 2350
Smithfield, NC 27577
www.johnston.cc.nc.us

Forsyth Technical
    Community College
2100 Silas Creek Pkwy.
Winston-Salem, NC 27103
www.forsyth.tec.nc.us

Nevada

Community College of
    Southern Nevada
6375 W. Charleston W1A
Las Vegas, NV 89146
www.ccsn.nevada.edu

Ohio

Mercy Medical Center
1320 Mercy Dr.
Canton, OH 44708
www.cantonmercy.com

Cincinnati State Technical
    and Community College
3250 Central Pkwy.
Cincinnati, OH 45247
www.cinstate.cc.oh.us

Lorain County Community
    College
1005 N. Abbe Rd.
Elyria, OH 44035
www.lorainccc.edu

Kettering College of Medical
    Arts
Diagnostic Medical
    Sonographer Program
3737 Southern Blvd.
Kettering, OH 45429
www.kcma.edu

Sanford Brown Institute
17535 Roubough Dr.
Middleburg Heights, OH
    44130
www.sbcleveland.com

Central Ohio Technical
    College
Diagnostic Medical
    Sonographer Program
1179 University Dr.
Newark, OH 43055
www.cotc.edu

Cuyahoga Community
    College
11000 Pleasant Valley Rd.
Parma, OH 44130
www.tri-c.cc.oh.us

Owens Community College
Diagnostic Medical
  Sonographer Program
P.O. Box 10,000
Toledo, OH 43699
www.owens.edu

Oklahoma

University of Oklahoma at
  Oklahoma City
Diagnostic Medical
  Sonographer Program
P.O. Box 26901, BMSB 357
Oklahoma City, OK 73190
www.medicine.ouhsc.edu

Pennsylvania

Northampton Community
  College
3835 Green Pond Rd.
Bethlehem, PA 18020
www.northampton.edu

College Misericordia
301 Lake St.
Dallas, PA 18612
www.misericordia.edu

Great Lakes Institute of
  Technology
5100 Peach St.
Erie, PA 16509
www.glit.org

Lancaster General College of
  Nursing and Health
  Sciences
410 North Lime St.
Lancaster, PA 17602
www.lancastergeneral.org

Community College of
  Allegheny County, Boyce
  Campus
Diagnostic Medical
  Sonographer Program
595 Beatty Rd.
Monroeville, PA 15146
www.ccac.edu

Thomas Jefferson University
Diagnostic Medical
  Sonographer Program
Philadelphia, PA 19107
www.jefferson.edu

Western School of Health and
  Business Careers
421 7th Ave.
Pittsburgh, PA 15219
www.western-school.com

Lackawanna College
501 Vine St.
Scranton, PA 18509
www.lackawanna.edu

Crozer-Chester Medical
  Center
1 Medical Center Blvd.
Upland, PA 19013
www.crozer.org

Wyoming Valley Health Care
  System-Hospital
575 N. River St.
Wilkes-Barre, PA 18764
www.wvhcs.org

Rhode Island

Rhode Island Hospital
3 Davol Sq., Bldg. A, 4th Fl.
Providence, RI 02903
www.lifespan.org/partners/rih

South Carolina

Greenville Technical College
P.O. Box 5616
Greenville, SC 29606
www.greenvilletech.com

Tennessee

Chattanooga State Technical
  Community College
4501 Amnicola Hwy.
Chattanooga, TN 37406
www.chattanoogastate.edu

Volunteer State Community
  College
1480 Nashville Pike
Gallatin, TN 37066
www.vscc.cc.tn.us

Baptist Memorial College of
  Health Sciences
1003 Monroe Ave., 3rd Fl.
Memphis, TN 38104
www.bchs.edu

Methodist Le Bonheur
  Healthcare
University Hospital
1265 Union Ave.
Memphis, TN 38104
www.methodisthealth.org

Vanderbilt University Medical
  Center
1161 21st Ave. S.
Nashville, TN 37232
www.mc.vanderbilt.edu

Texas

Austin Community College
Diagnostic Medical
   Sonographer Program
1020 Grove Blvd.
Austin, TX 78714
www.austin.cc.tx.us

Lamar University Institute of
   Technology, Beaumont
   Campus
P.O. Box 10061
Beaumont, TX 77710
www.theinstitute.lamar.edu

Del Mar College
Diagnostic Medical
   Sonographer Program
101 Baldwin
Corpus Christi, TX 78404
www.delmar.edu

Cy-Fair College
9191 Barker Cypress Rd.
Cypress, TX 77433
www.cy-faircollege.com

El Centro College
Diagnostic Medical
   Sonographer Program
Main & Lamar
Dallas, TX 75202
www.ecc.dcccd.edu

Sanford Brown Institute
2998 N. Stemmonds Freeway
Dallas, TX 75247
www.sbdallas.com

El Paso Community College
Diagnostic Medical
   Sonographer Program
P.O. Box 20500
El Paso, TX 79998
www.epcc.edu

Sanford Brown
   Institute–Houston
10500 Forum Pl. Dr., #200
Houston, TX 77036
www.sbhouston.com

Midland College
3600 N. Garfield
Midland, TX 79705
www.midland.edu

Tyler Junior College
P.O. Box 9020
Tyler, TX 75711
www.tjc.edu

Wharton County Junior
   College
911 Boling Hwy.
Wharton, TX 77488
www.wcjc.cc.tx.us

Virginia

Southwest Virginia
    Community College
P.O. Box SVCC
Richlands, VA 24641
www.sw.vccs.edu

Tidewater Community
    College
1700 College Crescent
Virginia Beach, VA 23456
www.tcc.edu

Washington

Bellevue Community College
Diagnostic Medical
    Sonographer Program
3000 Landerholm Circle SE,
    Rm. B243
Bellevue, WA 98007
www.bcc.ctc.edu

Seattle University
Diagnostic Medical
    Sonographer Program
900 Broadway and Madison
Seattle, WA 98122
www.seattleu.edu

West Virginia

Mountain State University
P.O. Box 9003
Beckley, WV
www.mountainstate.edu

West Virginia University
    Hospital
Diagnostic Medical
    Sonographer Program
P.O. Box 8062
Morgantown, WV 26506
www.wvuh.com

Wisconsin

Chippewa Valley Technical
    College
Diagnostic Medical
    Sonographer Program
620 W. Clairemont Ave.
Eau Claire, WI 54701
www.cvtc.edu

Northeast Wisconsin
    Technical College
2740 W. Mason St.
P.O. Box 19042
Green Bay, WI 54307
www.nwtc.edu

University of Wisconsin
   Hospital and Clinics
Department of Radiology
Diagnostic Medical
   Sonography Program
600 Highland Ave.
Madison, WI 53792
www.uwhealth.org

Columbia St. Mary's Hospital
2323 N. Lake Dr.
Milwaukee, WI 53201
www.columbia-stmarys.org

St. Francis Hospital
Diagnostic Medical
   Sonographer Program
3237 S. 16th St.
Milwaukee, WI 53215
www.stfrancishospitals.org

St. Luke's Medical Center
Diagnostic Medical
   Sonographer Program
AHC-Airport
Milwaukee, WI 53207
www.aurorahealthcare.org/faci
   lities/display.asp?id=0001

Professional Organizations

Accreditation

Commission on Accreditation of Allied Health Education
   Programs (CAAHEP)
35 E. Wacker Dr., Ste. 1970
Chicago, IL 60601
(312) 553-9355
www.caahep.org
CAAHEP accredits diagnostic medical sonographer programs.

Registration/Certification

American Chiropractic Registry of Radiologic
   Technologists (ACRRT)
2330 Gull Rd.
Kalamazoo, MI 49001
(269) 343-6666
www.acrrt.org

ACRRT is the national certifying agency for and registry of certified chiropractic radiologic technologists. ACRRT also educates the general public about the importance of having highly skilled radiologic technologists in chiropractic offices.

American Registry of Diagnostic Medical Sonographers (ARDMS)
51 Monroe St., Plaza East One
Rockville, MD 20850
(301) 738-8401
www.ardms.org

ARDMS is the national certifying agency for and registry of certified technologists in the field of diagnostic medical sonography and vascular technology. ARDMS publishes the *American Registry of Diagnostic Medical Sonographers Directory* (annual) and an *Informational Brochure* (annual).

American Registry of Radiologic Technologists (ARRT)
1255 Northland Dr.
Mendota Heights, MN 55120
(612) 687-0048
www.isrt.org/resources-arrt.htm

ARRT is the national certifying agency for and registry of certified radiographers, as well as nuclear medicine technologists and radiation therapy technologists, which are listed in the *ARRT Directory*. ARRT also offers advanced-level examinations in mammography and cardiovascular-interventional technology.

Nuclear Medicine Technology Certification Board (NMTCB)
2970 Clairmont Rd., Ste. 935
Atlanta, GA 30329
(404) 315-1739
www.nmtcb.org

NMTCB is the national certifying agency for and registry of certified nuclear medical technologists. NMTCB publishes the *Certification Examination Validation Report* (annual) and the *NMTCB Directory* (annual).

Professional Organizations—Imaging

American Society of Neuroimaging (ASN)
5841 Cedar Lake Rd., Ste. 204
Minneapolis, MN 55416
(952) 545-6291
www.asnweb.org

ASN holds an annual certification exam in computerized tomography and neurosonology and promotes the development of these techniques, as well as magnetic resonance imaging and other neurodiagnostic techniques. ASN encourages the collaboration of neurologists, neurosurgeons, neuroradiologists, and other scientists to improve these techniques through educational programs and scientific research.

Computerized Medical Imaging Society (CMIS)
c/o National Biomedical Research Foundation
Georgetown University Medical Center
3900 Reservoir Rd. NW
Washington, DC 20007
(202) 687-2121
www.rsna.org/orgs/cmis.html

CMIS provides a forum for physicians and other medical personnel to exchange information concerning the medical use of computerized tomography in radiological diagnosis. CMIS publishes *Computerized Medical Imaging and Graphics* (bimonthly).

Council on Diagnostic Imaging (CODI)
c/o American Chiropractic Association
1701 Clarendon Blvd.
Arlington, VA 22209
(800) 986-4636
www.amerchiro.org

CODI is the professional society of chiropractic roentgenologists, educators, students, and chiropractors who are interested in roentgenology.

Society of Computed Body Tomography and Magnetic Resonance
(SCBTMR)
c/o Matrix Meetings
P.O. Box 1026
Rochester, MN 55903-1026
(507) 288-5620
www.scbtmr.org

SCBTMR provides information on computed tomography and magnetic resonance imaging via lectures, workshops, seminars, and case presentations.

Society of Diagnostic Medical Sonographers (SDMS)
2745 Dallas Pkwy., Ste. 350
Plano, TX 75093-8730
(214) 473-8057
www.sdms.org

SDMS seeks to advance the science of diagnostic medical sonography; to establish and maintain high standards of education; and to provide an identity and sense of direction for members, which include sonographers, physician sonologists, and others who utilize high-frequency sound for diagnostic purposes. SDMS publishes the *Journal of Diagnostic Medical Sonography* (biennial).

Other Professional Organizations

American Association of Medical Dosimetrists (AAMD)
1 Physics Ellipse
College Park, MD 20740
(301) 209-3320
www.medicaldosimetry.org
AAMD publishes the *Medical Physics Journal.*

American Association for Women Radiologists (AAWR)
4550 Post Oak Pl., Ste. 342
Houston, TX 77027
(713) 965-0566
www.aawr.org
AAWR publishes a newsletter and a membership directory.

American Board of Nuclear Medicine (ABNM)
4555 Forest Park Blvd., Ste. 119
St. Louis, MO 63108
(314) 367-2225
www.abnm.org
ABNM is sponsored by the American Boards of Internal Medicine, Pathology, and Radiology, and the Society of Nuclear Medicine. It established requirements for specialty board certification for physicians in nuclear medicine. ABNM conducts examinations, issues certificates, and maintains a registry of certificate holders, as well as aids in the assessment and accreditation of nuclear medicine programs in hospitals and institutions offering graduate training. ABNM publishes the *American Board of Nuclear Medicine Information, Policies, and Procedures* (annual).

American Board of Radiology (ABR)
5441 E. Williams Blvd., Ste. 200
Tucson, AZ 85711
(520) 790-2900
www.theabr.org

ABR certifies physicians in the specialty of radiology and physicists in radiological physics and related branches by establishing qualifications and conducting examinations.

American College of Nuclear Medicine (ACNM)
101 W. Broad St., Ste. 614
Hazleton, PA 18201
(570) 501-9661
www.acnucmed.com

ACNM encourages improved and continuing education for practitioners in nuclear medicine, improving its benefits to patients and studying the socioeconomic aspects of the practice of nuclear medicine. ACNM bestows Gold Medal Awards and publishes the *ACNM Directory* (biennial) and *ACNM Report* (bimonthly).

American College of Nuclear Physicians (ACNP)
1850 Samuel Morse Dr.
Reston, VA 20190
(703) 326-1190
www.acnponline.org

ACNP seeks to foster the highest standards of nuclear medicine service and consultations to the public, hospitals, and referring physicians; to promote the continuing competence of practitioners of nuclear medicine; and to improve the socioeconomic aspects of the practice of nuclear medicine. ACNP publishes the *Directory* (annual) and *Scanner* (ten times a year).

American College of Podiatric Radiologists (ACPR)
169 Lincoln Rd., No. 308
Miami Beach, FL 33139
(305) 531-9866

ACPR is a professional society of podiatrists interested in the use and interpretation of X-rays in treating ailments of the lower extremities and publishes *Newsletter* (two to four times a year) and *Post Convention Reports* (one to two times a year).

American College of Radiology (ACR)
1891 Preston White Dr.
Reston, VA 20191
(703) 648-8900
www.acr.org

ACR is a professional society of physicians and radiologic physicists who specialize in the use of X-ray, ultrasound, nuclear medicine magnetic resonance, and other imaging modalities for the diagnosis of disease and treatment and management of cancer. ACR publishes books, booklets, pamphlets, textbooks, reprints, kits, films, and slides, and the *Bulletin* (monthly) and the *ACR Directory* (annual).

American Healthcare Radiology Administrators (AHRA)
490B Boston Post Rd., #101
Sudbury, MA 01776
(978) 443-7591
www.ahraonline.org

AHRA seeks to improve management of radiology departments in hospitals and other health care facilities and to provide a forum for publication of educational, scientific, and professional materials. AHRA publishes *Radiology Management* (quarterly) and *Bibliography for the Radiology Administrator.*

American Institute of Ultrasound in Medicine (AIUM)
14750 Sweitzer Ln., Ste. 100
Laurel, MD 20707
(301) 498-4100
www.aium.org

AIUM seeks to promote the application of ultrasound in clinical medicine, diagnosis, and research; study the effect of ultrasound on tissue; and recommend standards for its applications. AIUM publishes the *Journal of Ultrasound in Medicine* (monthly) and *AIUM Annual Convention Proceedings.* Also cited are: *American Institute of Ultrasound in Medicine—Official Book of Abstracts and Supplement to the Journal of Ultrasound in Medicine* (biennial), the *AIUM Newsletter* (monthly), and the *AIUM Membership Directory* (biennial).

American Osteopathic College of Radiology (AOCR)
119 E. 2nd St.
Milan, MO 63556
(660) 265-4011
www.aocr.org

AOCR is an organization that is composed of certified radiologists, residents-in-training, and others active in the field of radiology. It publishes the *AOCR Membership Directory* (annual) and *Viewbox* (quarterly).

American Radiological Nurses Association (ARNA)
7794 Grow Dr.
Pensacola, FL 32514
(850) 474-7292
www.arna.net

ARNA is an organization whose core purpose is to promote the growth of radiology nurses and advance standards of care.

American Roentgen Ray Society (ARRS)
44211 Slatestone Ct.
Leesburg, VA 20176-5109
(703) 648-8992
www.arrs.org

ARRS is an organization of specialists in diagnostic and/or therapeutic roentgenology. It publishes *American Journal of Roentgenology* (monthly) and the *ARRS Membership Directory* (annual).

American Society of Neuroradiology (ASNR)
2210 Midwest Rd., Ste. 207
Oak Brook, IL 60523
(630) 574-0220
www.asnr.org

ASNR seeks to foster education, basic science research, and communication in neuroradiology and publishes the *American Journal of Neuroradiology* (bimonthly) and the *ASNR Membership Roll* (annual).

American Society for Therapeutic Radiology and Oncology
   (ASTRO)
12500 Fair Lakes Circle, Ste. 375
Fairfax, VA 22033
(703) 502-1500
www.astro.org

ASTRO seeks to extend the benefits of radiation therapy to patients with cancer or other disorders, as well as to advance the scientific basis of radiation therapy. ASTRO publishes *The International Journal of Radiation Oncology, Biology, and Physics* (periodic), *ASTRO Membership Directory* (annual), and the *ASTRO Newsletter* (periodic).

Association of Educators in Radiological Sciences, Inc. (AERS)
P.O. Box 90204
Albuquerque, NM 87199
(505) 823-4740
www.aers.org
AERS publishes *Radiologic Science and Education.*

Association of University Radiologists (AUR)
820 Jorie Blvd.
Oak Brook, IL 60523
(630) 368-3730
www.aur.org
AUR seeks to provide a forum for university-based radiologists to present and discuss results of research, teaching, and administrative issues, as well as to encourage excellence in laboratory and clinical investigation and teaching. AUR publishes *Investigative Radiology* (monthly).

Conference of Radiation Control Program Directors (CRCPD)
205 Capital Ave.
Frankfort, KY 40601-2832
(502) 227-4543
www.crcpd.org
CRCPD seeks to promote radiological health and uniform radiation control laws and regulations; supports radiation control programs; provides assistance with members' technical work and development; and encourages cooperation between enforcement programs and agencies at state and federal levels. CRCPD publishes the *Directory of Personnel Responsible for Radiological Health*

Programs (annual), the *National Conference on Radiation Control Proceedings* (annual), the *Profile of State and Local Radiation Control Programs in the U.S.* (annual), and the *CRCPD Newsletter* (quarterly).

International Association of Dento-Maxillo-Facial Radiology
(IADMFR)
Prof. Dr. Robert P. Langlais
School of Dentistry
University of Texas HSC at San Antonio
7703 Floyd Curl Dr.
San Antonio, TX 78284
(210) 567-3333
www.iadmfr.org

IADMFR seeks to advance dento-maxillo-facial radiological research, teaching, and clinical service. IADMFR publishes the *Journal of Dento-Maxillo-Facial Radiology* (four times a year), the *Newsletter* (two times a year), and the *Proceedings* (triennial).

International Commission on Radiation Units and Measurements
(ICRU)
7910 Woodmont Ave., Ste. 800
Bethesda, MD 20814
(301) 657-2652
www.icru.org

ICRU develops internationally acceptable recommendations dealing with quantities and units of radiation and radionuclides, as well as procedures suitable for the measurement and application of these quantities in clinical radiology and radiobiology. ICRU publishes *ICRU Reports* (periodic).

International Organization for Medical Physics (IOMP)
www.iomp.org

IOMP publishes *Physics in Medicine and Biology, Clinical Physics and Physiological Measurement,* and *Medical Physics World.*

International Skeletal Society (ISS)
www.internationalskeletalsociety.com
ISS seeks to advance the science of skeletal radiology by bringing together radiologists and individuals in related disciplines and by providing continuing education courses. ISS publishes *Skeletal Radiology* (eight times a year), a *Membership Directory* (annual), and a *Newsletter* (three times a year).

International Society for Magnetic Resonance in Medicine, Inc.
   (ISMRM)
2118 Milvia St., Ste. 201
Berkeley, CA 94704
(510) 841-1899
www.ismrm.org
ISMRM was formed in 1993 as a merger between the Society of Magnetic Resonance in Medicine and the Society for Magnetic Resonance Imaging. It publishes *MR Pulse, Magnetic Resonance in Medicine,* and the *Journal of Magnetic Resonance Imaging.*

National Council on Radiation Protection and Measurements
   (NCRP)
7910 Woodmont Ave., Ste. 400
Bethesda, MD 20814
(301) 657-2652
www.ncrponline.org
(NCRP) formulates and disseminates recommendations on radiation protection and measurements based on the consensus of leading scientific thinking.

Radiological Society of North America (RSNA)

820 Jorie Blvd.

Oak Brook, IL 60523

630) 571-2670

www.rsna.org

RSNA promotes the study and practical application of radiology, radium, electricity, and other branches of physics related to medical science. It also publishes the *Directory of Members* (annual), *Radiographics* (bimonthly), and *RSNA Today* (bimonthly).

Society of Cardiovascular and Interventional Radiology (SCVIR)

10201 Lee Hwy., Ste. 500

Fairfax, VA 22030

(703) 691-1805

www.sirweb.org

SCVIR seeks to facilitate exchange of new ideas and techniques and provide educational courses for all physicians working in the field of cardiovascular and interventional radiology. SCVIR publishes the *Journal of Vascular and Interventional Radiology* (quarterly), the *SCVIR Membership Directory* (annual), the *SCVIR Newsletter* (bimonthly), the *Directory of Angiography and Interventional Radiology Fellowship Programs*, and *SCVIR News*.

Society of Nuclear Medicine (SNM)

1850 Samuel Morse Dr.

Reston, VA 20190

(703) 708-9000

http://interactive.snm.org

SNM disseminates information concerning the utilization of nuclear medicine, nuclear magnetic resonance, and the use of radioactive isotopes in the diagnosis and treatment of disease. SNM oversees the Technologist Section of the Society of Nuclear Medicine, as well as publishes the *Journal of Nuclear Medicine* (monthly) and the *Society of Nuclear Medicine Membership Directory* (every three years).

Society of Radiologists in Ultrasound (SRU)
44211 Slatestone Ct.
Leesburg, VA 20176
(703) 729-3353
www.sru.org

SRU seeks to advance the science, practice, and teaching of the specialty of ultrasound in radiology.

Appendix E

States That Require Licensure for the Practice of Radiologic Technology

Medical Radiological
   Technology Board of
   Examiners
4814 S. 40th St.
Phoenix, AZ 85040

Arkansas Department of
   Health
Radiologic Technology
   Licensure Program
4815 W. Markham St.
Little Rock, AR 72205

Department of Health
   Services
Radiological Health Branch
   Certification
P.O. Box 997414, MS #7610
Sacramento, CA 95899

Colorado State Medical Board
1560 Broadway, Ste. 1300
Denver, CO 80202

Department of Public Health
Bureau of Health System
   Regulation
410 Capitol Ave.
MS #12APP
Hartford, CT 06134

Office of Radiation Control
Jesse Cooper Bldg.
P.O. Box 637
Dover, DE 19903

Office of Radiation Control
4025 Bald Cypress Way
Bin C21
Tallahassee, FL 32399

Noise and Radiation Branch
591 Ala Moana Blvd.
P.O. Box 3378
Honolulu, HI 96813-2498

Illinois Emergency
    Management Agency
Division of Nuclear Safety
1035 Outer Park Dr.
Springfield, IL 62704

Indiana State Board of Health
Radiological Health Division
    Director
2 N. Meridian St., 5F
Indianapolis, IN 46204

Iowa State Department of
    Health
Bureau of Environmental
    Health
401 SW 7th St., Ste. D
Des Moines, IA 50309

Department of Health
    Services
Radiation Control Branch
275 E. Main St.
Frankfort, KY 40621

Louisiana State Radiologic
    Technology
Board of Examiners
3108 Cleary Ave., Ste. 207
Metairie, LA 70002

Radiologic Technology
Board of Examiners
State House Station #35
Augusta, ME 04333

Maryland Board of Physician
    Quality Assurance
4201 Patterson Ave.
P.O. Box 2571
Baltimore, MD 21215

Department of Public Health
Radiation Control Program
90 Washington St.
Dorchester, MA 02121

Department of Health
Radiation Control Section
1645 Energy Park Dr., Ste.
    300
St. Paul, MN 55108

State Department of Health
Professional Licensure
P.O. Box 1700
Jackson, MS 39215

Montana Board of Radiologic
Technologists
301 S. Park, 4th Fl.
Helena, MT 59620

Professional & Occupational
Licensure Division
301 Centennial Mall South
Lincoln, NE 68509

Bureau of Radiological Health
CN415
Trenton, NJ 08625

Radiologic Technologist
Program
P.O. Box 26110
Santa Fe, NM 87502

New York State Dept. of
Health
Bureau of Environmental
Radiation Protection
547 River St., Rm. 530
Troy, NY 12180

Ohio Department of
Radiological Technology
Section
246 N. High St.
Columbus, OH 43266

Board of Radiologic
Technology
800 NE Oregon St., Ste.
1160A
Portland, OR 97232

Bureau of Professional and
Occupational Affairs
State Board of Medicine
P.O. Box 2649
Harrisburg, PA 17105

Rhode Island Department of
Health
Division of Professional
Regulations
3 Capitol Hill
Providence, RI 02908

South Carolina Radiation
Quality Standards
Association
P.O. Box 7515
Columbia, SC 29202

Tennessee Board of Medical
Examiners
425 5th Ave., 1st Fl.
Cordell Hull Bldg.
Nashville, TN 37247

Texas Department of Health
Professional Licensing &
  Certification Division
1100 W. 49th St.
Austin, TX 78756

Bureau of Health Professions
Division of Occupational and
  Professional Licensing
160 E. 300 S.
P.O. Box 45805
Salt Lake City, UT 84144

Board of Radiologic
  Technology
Office of the Secretary of
  State
26 Terrance St.
Montpelier, VT 05609

Department of Health
  Professions
6603 W. Broad St., 5th Fl.
Richmond, VA 23230

Radiologic Technologist
  Program
P.O. Box 47869
Olympia, WA 98504

West Virginia Radiologic
  Technology
Board of Examiners
1715 Flat Top Rd.
Cool Ridge, WV 25825

The State of Wyoming
Board of Radiologic
  Technologists Examiners
2020 Carey Ave.
First Bank Plaza, Ste. 201
Cheyenne, WY 82002

GLOSSARY

Aliasing Interference caused by beats or signals between the emitted and received signals of a Doppler ultrasound system.

Alpha particle A group of four particles (two protons and two neutrons) emitted from an unstable nucleus.

Alpha ray A stream of alpha particles emitted from a large group of unstable nuclei.

Annular array A group of transducers, antennas, or other detectors arranged in an annulus (ring).

Attenuation The decrease in dose rate of radiation passing through a material.

Background radiation In a given area, the sum total of radioactivity from cosmic rays, natural radioactive materials, and whatever may have been introduced into the area.

Becquerd (Bg) A unit of radioactive material. Thirty-seven billion curies equal one becquerd.

Charge An ionized particle. If an electron is removed from an atom, two charges are formed. The displaced electron is the negative charge, and the rest of the atom is the positive charge. Sometimes the electron becomes attached to an otherwise neutral atom, thus giving the atom a negative charge.

Coil Single or multiple loops of wire (or other electrical conductor, such as tubing) designed either to produce a magnetic field from current flowing through the wire, or to detect a changing magnetic field by voltage induced in the wire.

Continuous wave (CW) NMR A technique for studying nuclear magnetic resonance (NMR) by continuously inputting radiofrequency radiation to the sample and applying either the total range of radiation frequencies or the magnetic field through the total range of resonance values; this technique has been largely superseded by pulse NMR techniques.

Contrast The relative difference of the signal intensities in two adjacent regions.

Curie (Ci) A unit of radioactive material.

Decay The transformation of one element into another by the emission of alpha or beta particles from the nucleus.

Diamagnetic material A substance that is repelled by magnetism.

Dielectric material A substance that insulates two conductors of electricity from each other.

Dielectric constant A number indicating the efficiency of a dielectric as an insulator. The higher the number, the greater the efficiency.

Direct ionization Ionization brought about by the direct action of the ionizing cause.

Eddy current An induced electric current circulating through the entire body of a mass. Such currents are converted into heat, causing serious waste.

Electromagnet A magnet created by passing an electric current through a coil of wire. A core of magnetic material is placed in the center of the coil to concentrate the magnetic field.

Electromagnetic spectrum The range of energies of electromagnetic radiations.

Electromagnetic wave A wave produced by the oscillation of an electric charge.

Electron volt (eV) An energy unit; the amount of energy acquired when an electron falls through a potential difference of one volt.

emf Electromotive force. Other names are potential difference and voltage.

Endoscopic Refers to the examination of a body cavity by means of an instrument.

Ferromagnetic material Material that makes a good magnet.

Field An area of influence.

Fourier transform A mathematical procedure to separate the frequency components of a signal from its amplitudes as a function of time. The Fourier transform is used to generate the spectrum from the time domain data in pulse nuclear magnetic resonance techniques and is essential to most imaging techniques.

Frequency (FT) The number of vibrations or cycles in a unit of time. For electromagnetic radiation, such as radio waves, the old unit cycles per second (cps) has been replaced by the SI unit hertz (Hz).

Gamma ray When an unstable nucleus has emitted an alpha or beta particle, it is often left with excess energy. This is given out as a gamma ray. It is usually associated with beta emission rather than alpha emission.

Gauss (G) A unit of magnetic flux density in the metric system. The earth's magnetic field is approximately 0.5 gauss, depending on location. The currently preferred (SI) unit is the tesla. One tesla equals ten thousand gauss.

Gradient magnetic field A magnetic field that changes in strength along a certain given direction.

Ground The earth (or ground) is regarded as a huge reservoir of electrons. Any charged body that is connected to ground will become neutralized.

Half-life The time taken for the radioactivity of a radioisotope to decay to half its original value.

Hertz A measurement of frequency. One hertz equals one cycle per second.

Hysteresis A lagging or retardation of the effect, such as when the magnetization of a piece of iron or steel, caused by a magnetic field that varies through a cycle of values, lags behind the field.

Indirect ionization Ionization caused secondarily to the action of the original ionizing influence, not by the original ionizing influence itself.

Insulator A substance that tends to oppose the passage of electric current.

Inverse square law The intensity of radiation at any point is inversely proportional to the square of the distance of that point from the source of radiation.

Ionization Ionization occurs when an electron is removed from the orbit of a neutral atom and the atom is left with an overall positive charge. The positively charged atom is called a positive ion, and the electron is called a negative ion.

Ionizing radiation Any form of radiation that causes ionization; for example, alpha rays, beta rays, X-rays, and gamma rays.

Isotope Of a collection of atoms of a given element (that is, having the same number of protons), those atoms possessing a different number of neutrons are the different isotopes of the element.

Kilohertz (kHz) Unit of frequency.

Magnetic dipole North and south magnetic poles, separated by a finite distance.

Magnetic field (H) The region surrounding a magnet (or current-carrying conductor). It is endowed with certain properties; one is that a small magnet in such a region experiences a torque that tends to align it in a given direction.

Magnetic induction (B) The net magnetic effect from an externally applied magnetic field and the resulting magnetization. Also called magnetic flux density.

MegaHertz (MHz) Unit of frequency.

Neutron A nuclear particle the size of a proton, but carrying no charge.

Nonmagnetic material Material that cannot be magnetized.

Nuclear decay An unstable nucleus, such as in a radioactive isotope, will attempt to reach a stable state by emitting an alpha particle or by "splitting" a proton or neutron and emitting a beta particle. In the process, its chemical identity is altered.

Nucleus The central part of an atom containing most of the mass of the atom. It is made of protons and neutrons.

Paramagnetic material Material that can be magnetized, but only with difficulty and only weakly.

Permeability The ease with which a material can be magnetized or demagnetized. Substances with high permeability are easy to magnetize, and those with low permeability are hard.

Piezoelectric transducer A device for converting electric energy into mechanical and vice versa.

Pixel Acronym for a picture element; the smallest discrete part of a digital image display.

Positron An unnatural particle the same size as an electron, but carrying a positive charge instead of a negative charge. This particle is manufactured in certain processes of nuclear decay and soon becomes converted to some other form of energy.

Potential difference The energy available to move a current around an electrical circuit. It is the difference in energy between a point at a high negative potential and some other point at a low negative potential. If the two points are connected to each other, electrons will move from the high negative potential to the low; this constitutes a current flow.

Precession Comparatively slow gyration of the axis of a spinning body so as to trace out a cone, caused by the application of a torque tending to change the direction of the rotation axis.

Proton A nuclear particle the same size as a neutron and carrying a positive charge. It is approximately 1,850 times larger than an electron.

Rad A unit of radiation. The corresponding SI unit is the gray (abbreviated Gy).

Radioactive isotope An unstable isotope. In such an isotope, the nucleus tries to reach a stable state by the emission of a particle and, sometimes, energy.

Rem A unit of radiation. The corresponding SI unit is the sievert (abbreviated Sv).

Roentgen A unit of measure of an X-ray; the amount of conductivity of one milliliter of atmospheric air (at saturation) at zero degrees Celsius and 760 millimeters of mercury pressure. For X-rays, as used in diagnostic radiology, one roentgen equals one rad equals one rem. This relationship may not be true for other radiation sources.

SI Abbreviation for systeme internationale d'units, the system of measurements accepted by scientists worldwide. It is similar, but not identical, to the metric system.

Static discharge When the potential difference between two electrodes separated by an insulating material becomes great enough, the surplus electrons on the negative electrode cross the gap to the positive electrode in one big burst.

Wavelength The distance from a particular point on a wave to the same point on the next wave; for example, from the crest of one wave to the crest of the next.

X-ray A form of electromagnetic radiation.

About the Author

Dr. Clifford J. Sherry has spent the last thirty-five years in a variety of settings learning to identify problems and finding methods and procedures to solve them. He has been involved in the conception, preparation, execution, and presentation of basic and applied research. He has professional publications in more than twenty-five different referenced scientific journals. Much of this research has focused on how the nervous system processes information. In addition to his work in neurophysiology, Sherry also has worked and published in the areas of psychopharmacology, reproductive behavior/physiology, teratology, and the biobehavioral effects of electromagnetic fields and acoustics.

Sherry has taught human physiology and psychopharmacology, as well as perception and theories of learning, to more than two thousand students of widely varying backgrounds and abilities. He has presented his ideas to lay and professional audiences via public speeches, lectures, and workshops. He has an ever-increasing number of articles in magazines that focus on, but are not limited to, making science, medicine, computers, and the law understandable to nonspecialists. His books include *Contemporary World Issues Endangered Species* and *Contemporary World Issues Animal Rights*, both with ABC-CLIO, Santa Barbara, CA; *The New Science of Technical Analysis Using the Statistical Techniques of Neuroscience to Uncover Order and Chaos in the Markets* and *Mathematics of Technical Analysis Applying Statistics to Trading Stocks, Options, and Futures*, both republished with iUniverse.com; and *Inhalants and Drugs* and *Eating Disorders*, both with Rosen Publishing Group, New York.